WATCHWORDS

FOR THE

WARFARE OF LIFE.

FROM DR. MARTIN LUTHER.

TRANSLATED AND ARRANGED BY THE AUTHOR OF
"CHRONICLES OF THE SCHONBERG-COTTA FAMILY."

„Euer Leben ist eine Ritterschaft."
MARTIN LUTHER.

NEW YORK:
M. W. DODD, 506 BROADWAY.
1869.

This scarce antiquarian book is included in our special *Legacy Reprint Series*. In the interest of creating a more extensive selection of rare historical book reprints, we have chosen to reproduce this title even though it may possibly have occasional imperfections such as missing and blurred pages, missing text, poor pictures, markings, dark backgrounds and other reproduction issues beyond our control. Because this work is culturally important, we have made it available as a part of our commitment to protecting, preserving and promoting the world's literature.

TO THE

𝔐𝔬𝔰𝔱 𝔟𝔢𝔩𝔬𝔳𝔢𝔡 𝔐𝔢𝔪𝔬𝔯𝔶 𝔬𝔣 𝔒𝔫𝔢

WHO

FOUGHT A GOOD FIGHT AND ENDURED TO THE END

AND

overcame and now liveth unto God, more than Conqueror through Him that loved us ;

SERVING HIM AND SEEING HIS FACE

FOREVER.

LUTHER'S Prose is a half-battle; few deeds are equal to his words.

"Look up to this evergreen Oak and its branches; to this Tower, which, if not always a light-house, was always a church-tower with its alarm-bells and its friendly peals.

"Every brave life appears to us out of the past not so brave as it really was, for the forms of terror with which it fought are overthrown. Against the many-armed Future threatening from its clouds, only the great soul has courage; every one can be courageous towards the spent-out, disclothed Past. Luther stood in the midst of the electric tempests which he had enkindled, and for us cleared and unfolded them into pure air."

JEAN PAUL FRIEDRICH RICHTER.

I did greatly long to see some ancient godly man's experience who had writ some hundreds of years before I was born, for those who had writ in our days, I thought, had only writ that which others had felt, or else had through the strength of their wits and parts studied to answer such objections as they perceived others were perplexed with, without going themselves down into the deep. Well, after many such longings in my mind, the God in whose hands are all our days and ways, did cast into my hand one day a book of Martin Luther. It was his Commentary on the Galatians; it also was so old that it was ready to fall piece from piece, if I did but turn it over. Then I was pleased much that such an old book had fallen into my hands; the which, when I had but a little way perused, I found my condition, in his experience, so largely and profoundly handled, as if this book had been written out of my heart. This made me marvel; for this man, I thought, could not know anything of the state of Christians now, but must thus write of the experience of former days. This, therefore, I must let fall before all men, I do prefer this book of Martin Luther on the Galatians, excepting the Holy Bible, before all the books that ever I have seen as most fit for a wounded conscience.

JOHN BUNYAN.

INTRODUCTORY NOTE.

THE selections in this volume have all been freshly translated from Luther's own German or Latin, with the exception of the extracts taken from the sixteenth century translation of the Commentary on the Galatians.

The majority of the extracts are from the Letters and the Tischreden.

THE AUTHOR.

CONTENTS.

Part 1.

WORDS FOR THE BATTLE-FIELD.

I.
THE COMMANDER.............................. 17
II.
RULES OF THE SERVICE........................ 42
III.
THE WEAPONS OF OUR WARFARE................. 55
IV.
THE ARMIES OF HEAVEN....................... 100
V.
THE ENEMY................................. 110

CONTENTS.

Part 2.

WORDS FOR THE DAY'S MARCH.

I.
THE LEADER.................................155
II.
SPECIAL GRACES............................165

Part 3.

WORDS FOR THE HALTING-PLACES.

I.
THE VISIBLE CREATION......................191
II.
THE HOLY SCRIPTURES......................205
III.
THE FATHERS AND DOCTORS OF THE CHURCH......220
IV.
HEROES....................................223
V.
CHILDREN..................................229
VI.
MUSIC.....................................236

Part 4.

WORDS FOR THE WOUNDED.

I.
Trial of Various Kinds..................243

II.
Sickness.........................255

III.
Bereavement....................266

Part 5.

WORDS OF VICTORY.

I.
The Last Conflict........ 295

II.
The Present Life of the Just in Heaven.......306

III.
The Resurrection and the Glorious Advent...315

THE BATTLE-FIELD.

I.

THE COMMANDER.

We must strive, for we are under one Lord of armies and Prince of warriors. Therefore, with one hand we must build, and in the other bear the sword.

It must not be "*Sic ego Philippus.*" The "ego" is too small. The word is, "*I am that I am.*

LOVE is an image of God, and not a lifeless image, nor one painted on paper, but the living essence of the Divine Nature, which beams full of all goodness.

He is not harsh, as we are to those who have injured us. We withdraw our hand and close our purse; but He is kind to the unthankful and the evil.

He sees thee in thy poverty and wretchedness, and knows thou hast nothing to pay; therefore He freely forgives and gives thee all.

"GOD'S love gives in such a way, that it flows from a Father's heart, the well-spring of all good. The heart of the giver makes the gift dear and precious ; as among ourselves we say of even a trifling gift, 'It comes from a hand we love,' and look not so much at the gift as at the heart."

"IF we will only consider Him in His works, we shall learn that God is nothing else but pure, unutterable love, greater and more than any one can think. The shameful thing is, that the world does not regard this, nor thank Him for it, although every day it sees before it such countless benefits from Him ; and it deserves for its ingratitude that the sun should not shine another moment longer, nor the grass grow ; yet He ceases not, for one moment's interval, to love us and to do us good. Language must fail me to speak of His spiritual gifts. Here He pours forth for us, not sun and moon, nor heaven and earth, but His own heart, His beloved Son, so that He suffered His blood to be shed, and the most shameful death to be inflicted on Him, for us wretched, wicked, thankless creatures. How, then, can we say anything but that God is an abyss of endless, unfathomable love ? "

"THE whole Bible is full of this—that we should not doubt, but be absolutely certain, that God is merciful, gracious, patient, faithful, and true; who not only will keep His promises, but already has kept and done abundantly beyond what He promised, since He has given His own Son for our sins on the cross, that all who believe on Him should not perish, but have everlasting life."

"WHOEVER believes, and embraces this, that God has given His only Son to die for us poor sinners, to him it is no longer any doubt, but the most certain truth, that God reconciles us to Himself, and is favorable and heartily gracious to us."

"SINCE the gospel shows us Christ the Son of God, who, according to the will of the Father, has offered Himself for us, and has satisfied for sin, the heart can no more doubt God's goodness and grace—is no more affrighted, nor flies from God, but sets all its hope in His goodness and mercy."

THE apostles are always exhorting us to continue in the love of God—that is, that each one should entirely conclude in his heart that he is loved by God; and they set before our eyes a certain proof of it, in that God has not spared His Son, but given Him for the world, that through His death the world might again have life.

It is God's honor and glory to give liberally.

His nature is all pure love, so that if any one would describe or picture God, he must describe One who is pure love, the Divine Nature being nothing else than a furnace and glow of such love that it fills heaven and earth.

IT is not to be borne that Christian people should say, We cannot know whether God is favorable to us or not. On the contrary, we should learn to say, I know that I believe in Christ, and therefore that God is my gracious Father.

WHAT is the reason that God gives? What moves Him to it? Nothing but unutterable love, because He delights to give and to bless. What does He give? Not empires merely, not a world full of silver and gold, not heaven and earth only; but His Son, who is as great as Himself —that is, eternal and incomprehensible, a Gift as infinite as the Giver, the very spring and fountain of all grace; yea, the possession and property of all the riches and treasures of God.

Omnipresence.

GOD is limited to no place. He is also excluded from none. He is in all places, and in the least of His creatures, in the petal of the flower, in a blade of grass; and yet He is in no place. Nowhere, comprehensively and exclusively; everywhere, because everywhere He is creating and upholding everything.

The Creation not Left to Itself.

GOD has not so created the creatures that after creating He abandons them. He loves them, delights in them, is with them; moves and sustains each creature according to its kind.

We Christians know that with God creating and sustaining are one thing.

The Creator.

TO Magister Holflein, Doctor Martin Luther said, "Dear Master, where were you, sixty years ago? Where was I? Whence came I hither? Whence came you hither? We did not create ourselves, and yet, now, we want to go to our Lord God and bargain with Him, and sell Him our works! He must, forsooth, give us His heaven for them! Is not this a shameful thing, that a creature should lift itself up thus and desire to traffic with its Creator?

"We do not really believe that God is our Creator. If we believed it, we should act far otherwise. But no one believes that God is the Creator. Even when we say it, and our conscience convinces us, it is not genuine earnest with us.

"We virtually go up to God and say, 'Lord

God, look on me for my works' sake! I come to Thee. Thou hast not created me.' Shame on us."

The Living God.

THE chief thing that God requireth of man is that he giveth unto Him the glory of His Divinity—that is to say, that he taketh Him not for an idol, but for God, who looketh on him, listeneth to him, showeth mercy on him, and helpeth.

" True Christian Divinity."

TRUE Christian Divinity setteth not God forth unto us in His Majesty. It commandeth us not to search out the nature of God, but to know His will set forth to us in Christ.

Therefore begin thou where Christ began—namely, in the womb of the Virgin, in the manger, and at His mother's breast. It is to this end He came down, was born, was conversant among men; suffered, was crucified and died, that by all means He might set Himself forth plainly before us, and fasten the eyes of our heart upon Himself, that He might thereby keep us from climbing up into heaven, and from the curious searching of the Divine Majesty.

Christ Revealing the Father.

CHRIST, according to His office, calleth us back unto the Father's will, that in His words and works we should not so much look on Him, but on the Father. For Christ came into this world, and took man's nature on Him, that He might be a sacrifice for the sins of the whole world, and so reconcile us to God the Father; that He alone might declare unto us how this was done through the good pleasure of the Father, that we, by fastening our eyes on Christ, might be drawn and carried straight unto the Father.

Theology Beginning at Bethlehem.

CHRISTIAN religion beginneth not at the highest, as other religions do, but at the lowest. It will have us to climb up by Jacob's ladder, whereupon God Himself leaneth, whose feet touch the very earth, hard by the head of Jacob.

Run straight to the manger, and embrace this infant, the Virgin's little babe, in thine arms; and behold Him as He was born, nursed, grew up, was conversant amongst men; teaching; dying; rising again; ascending up above all the heavens, and having power over all things.

This sight and contemplation will keep thee in the right way, that thou mayest follow whither Christ hath gone.

God Stooping to Man.

THE Gospel is the Revelation of the Son of God.

With our reason we can never comprehend what God the Creator is. And for this cause He has taught, "It is in vain; human reason cannot comprehend Me. I am too great and too high. I will make Myself little, that man may understand Me; I will give him My Son, and so give Him, that for man He shall become a sacrifice, sin and a curse, and be obedient to Me the Father, even to the death of the cross."

This is indeed to become little and comprehensible. But who believes it? *Novem ubi sunt?* "Where are the nine?"

The Incarnation.

IN deep spiritual temptations nothing has helped me better, with nothing have I heartened myself and driven away the devil better than with this, that Christ, the true Eternal Son of God, is "bone of our bone, and flesh of our flesh," and that he sits on the right hand of God, and pleads for us. When I can grasp this shield of faith, I have already chased away the evil one with his fiery darts.

ANNO Domini 1538, on the 25th of December, on Christmas Day, Doctor Martin Luther was very joyous, and all his sayings, songs, and thoughts were about the Incarnation of Christ our Saviour. And he said, with a deep sigh,—

"Ah, we poor human creatures, how coldly and tamely we greet this great joy which has come to bless us! This is the great act of beneficence which far excels all other works of creation. And shall we so feebly believe it, when it has been announced to us, preached, and sung by the angels? (heavenly theologians and preachers, indeed!) And they have rejoiced on our account, and their song is verily a glorious song, wherein is briefly enfolded the sum of the whole Christian religion. For the *Gloria in excelsis Deo*, 'Glory to God in the highest,' is the highest worship, and this they bring to us in this Christ.

"For the world since Adam's fall knows neither God nor His creatures; lives without regarding God's glory; praises, honors, glorifies Him not. Oh, what choice, joyous thoughts man would have had; seeing even in the lowliest flowers that our Lord God is an Artist and Master whom none can imitate!

"Wherefore the dear angels call us, fallen creatures, to faith in Christ, and to love; that we, giving glory to God alone, may have peace in this life, both with God and with one another."

THE Feast of the Annunciation may well be called the Feast of the Incarnation. Then our Redemption began. Thus the French and the English date the beginning of the year from this Feast. For this mystery no one can explain, nor fathom with his reason, that God, the Highest Majesty, has humbled Himself to take on Him our flesh.

On this day we preachers should diligently picture to the people the History of the Festival, as Luke describes it, circumstantially and in order; and we should, all together, have joy and delight in the comforting, blessed story that, as on this day, Christ our Lord and Saviour, conceived by the Holy Ghost, took our human nature upon Him, of the pure chaste Virgin Mary; became our Brother; lifted up our condemned and corrupted humanity to this highest glory, that we should be children of God, and His fellow-heirs, at which, indeed, we should rejoice more than over all the treasures of this earth.

It is true we cannot enough praise Mary, that high, noble creature; but when the Creator Himself comes and gives Himself for us, to redeem us from the power of the devil, for this inexpressible grace, neither we nor the angels can praise and bless Him enough to eternity.

The Childhood and Youth of our Lord.

ALL the wisdom of the world is mere child's play, yes, folly, compared with the knowledge of Christ. For what is more wonderful than to know and acknowledge the great, unspeakable mystery that the Son of God, the express Image of the Eternal Father, has taken our nature on Him, and become in fashion as a man?

At Nazareth He must have helped His father

build houses; for Joseph was a carpenter. Therefore Christ was called "the carpenter's son;" yes, Himself "the carpenter."

What will the people of Nazareth think at the Last Day, when they shall see Christ sitting in Divine Majesty, and may say to Him, "Lord, didst Thou not help build my house? How then comest Thou to this high glory?"

Many fables have been imaged, by many, of what Jesus did in His childhood and youth, as can be seen in the book with the title, "*De Infanti à Salvatoris*," and "*De Vita Jesu*." But because in this book stands many a foolish, ridiculous thing, it has never been esteemed by Christians.

This, however, is the needful thing, that we Christians should with all diligence learn and know that the Son of God did so deeply humble Himself, was born so poor and in such a low estate, all on account of our sins; and that for our sakes He hid His Majesty so long.

When He was born, He wept and wailed like another babe. Mary had to wait on Him and tend Him, and feed Him at her breast (as the Church sings, "A little milk was once His food"), to cherish, clothe, lift, and carry Him, lay Him to rest, as any other mother her babe.

Soon afterwards Joseph, with the mother and the babe, in distress, had to flee into Egypt, from Herod.

When, after Herod's death, they came back to

Nazareth, He was subject to His parents, and no doubt often brought them bread, drink, and other things. Mary may have said to Him, "Jesus, where hast Thou been? Canst Thou not stay at home!" And when He grew up, He must have helped Joseph at the carpentering, &c. Not to stumble nor to be offended at this feeble, lowly form, this despised mode of life, which was seen in Christ, is great, high art and wisdom, yea, God's gift, and the Holy Ghost's own work.

Some are offended because we sometimes say in the pulpit that Christ was a carpenter (Zimmergesell). But it is a far greater offence that He was nailed to the cross, as one guilty of blasphemy and insurrection, between two malefactors.

IT is written that there was once a pious godly bishop who had often earnestly prayed that God would manifest to him what Jesus had done in his youth. Once the bishop had a dream to this effect. He seemed, in his sleep, to see a carpenter working at his trade, and beside him a little boy, who was gathering up chips. Then came in a maiden, clothed in green, who called them both to come to the meal, and set porridge (Brei) before them. All this the bishop seemed to see in his dream, himself standing behind the door that he might not be perceived. Then the little boy began and said, "Why does that man stand there? Shall not he also eat with us?" And this so frightened the bishop that he awoke.

Let this be what it may, a true history or a fable, I none the less believe that Christ in His childhood and youth looked and acted like other children, "yet without sin," "in fashion like a man."

Often (so I think, I assert it not for truth), when His parents had need, by His Divine power He may have created and brought them what they needed, without money. For when His mother saw at the marriage-feast at Cana that they wanted wine, from her motherly heart she said to Him with confidence, "They have no wine," as if often before she had seen how He could help in need.

Whosoever, therefore, will rightly comprehend this child, must think that there is no higher wisdom than to acknowledge Christ, and not to be offended or turned aside, because the world holds all this for the greatest foolishness. For to us who believe it is the "wisdom of God and the power of God" whereby we are saved, and wherein the dear angels have delight and joy.

Therefore it pleases me very well, when in the churches they sing aloud, and with a solemn slowness, *Et homo factus est* and *Verbum caro factum est*. To these words the devil cannot listen, but must flee many miles from them, for he feels well what there is in them.

If we rejoiced from our hearts over those

words, as the devil trembles at them, it would be well for us.

Christ at the Judgment-Seat.

IS it not a wonderful thing that the Son of God should sit there and suffer himself to be so piteously tormented, scorned, and mocked?—He whom all angels adore, before whom the earth trembles?—Whom all the creatures acknowledge as their Creator, in His face they spit, strike Him on the lips with a reed, say in mockery, "Ah, if He is a king He must have a crown and sceptre!"

Oh, our sufferings are nothing! When I think of them, I am ashamed to death. Yet we are to be conformed to the image of the Son of God; and if our sufferings could be as great as His, it would still be nothing in comparison. For He is the Son of God, and we are poor creatures. If we suffered eternal death, it were nothing in comparison.

The Last Supper.

THE supper which Christ held with His disciples when He gave them His farewell must have been full of friendly heart-intercourse; for Christ spoke just as tenderly and cordially to them as a father to his dear little children when he is obliged to part from them. He made the best of their infirmities, and had patience with them, although all the while they were so slow to understand, and still lisped like babes.

Yet that must indeed have been choice, friendly, and delightful converse when Philip said, " Show us the Father ; " and Thomas, " We know not the way ; " and Peter, " I will go with Thee to prison and to death."

It was simple, quiet table-talk ; every one opening his heart and showing his thoughts freely and fearlessly, and without restraint.

Never since the world began was there a more delightful meal than that.

The Agony in the Garden.

DR. LUTHER was once questioned at table concerning the "bloody sweat," and the other deep spiritual sufferings which Christ endured in the garden. Then he said—"No man can know or conceive what that anguish must have been. If any man began even to experience such suffering, he must die. You know many do die of sickness of heart ; for heart-anguish is indeed death. If a man could feel such anguish and distress as Christ felt, it would be impossible for him to endure it and for his soul to remain in his body. Soul and body would part. To Christ alone was this agony possible, and it wrung from Him 'sweat which was as great drops of blood.'"

The Ascension of Christ.

A WONDERFUL thing it must have been to see, when Christ vanished before the disciples' eyes, and went up into heaven. The good disciples must have thought, "We have eaten and drunk with Him, and now, whilst looking at us, He is taken from us into heaven."

I know Dr. Justus Jonas very intimately, and if he were now raised up into heaven, and were to vanish before our eyes, it would give us many strange and wonderful thoughts.

"*NO man hath ascended into heaven save He who came down from heaven, even the Son of Man, who is in heaven.*"

In these three sayings are briefly comprehended His almightiness. "To come down from heaven," means that He appeared on earth, became man (in all things like us, save in sin), let His glory be seen in his words and wondrous works, and at last accomplished the redemption of the human race.

"To ascend to heaven," means that henceforth He appears no more on earth in bodily form.

"Is in heaven," means that in His Godhead He has never left the right hand of the Father, and moreover that He has never relinquished, and will never relinquish, the human nature which He has taken on Him.

The Holy Spirit.

ON the Day of Pentecost the Holy Spirit began the New Testament. Then He openly established his office and work, as Christ proclaimed Him, " the Comforter, and the Spirit of Truth."

For He gave to the apostles and disciples a true, sure consolation in their hearts, and an assured, joyful mind, so that they did not ask if the world and the devil were favorable or unfavorable, raged or laughed, but went through the streets of the city, and thought, " Here neither Annas, Caiaphas, Pilate, or Herod are anything. We Christians are all. All are our subjects and servants, and we their lords and rulers."

That these poor beggars and fishermen, the apostles, should step forth and preach as they did, enraging the whole government at Jerusalem, bringing on themselves the wrath of the priests also, and of the whole Roman empire, opening their mouths and crying, " Ye are traitors and murderers," knowing that they would in consequence be smitten on the mouth ; all this could not have been but through the Holy Spirit.

THE Holy Ghost is called the Comforter, not one who makes sad; for where melancholy and depression are, there the Holy Ghost, the Comforter, is not at home. The devil is a spirit of terror and sadness. But the Holy Ghost is the Comforter.

THE Holy Ghost, who is called a Witness and a Comforter, preaches and testifies throughout Christendom, to comfort and strengthen all the sorrowful, of none save only of Christ.

THE Holy Scriptures give to the Holy Spirit a very choice name, calling Him an Advocate, Paraclete, who conducts our cause and does the best for us, speaks for us, makes intercession for us, and helps us up again when we are fallen. Thus we obtain the victory through faith, and overcome the devil and the world, not by our own means and powers, but by the power and working of the Holy Spirit and of faith.

The Love of God.

THE slender capacity of man's heart cannot comprehend, much less utter, that unsearchable depth and burning zeal of God's love towards us.

God is gracious and merciful, as the Scriptures show. He loves even real sinners (bösen Buben). Yea, to the blind, hard world which lieth in the wicked one, He has sent as a Saviour His own Son. I could not have done that, and yet I am a real sinner (böse Bube) myself.

"True Definition of Christ."

FOR, indeed, Christ is no cruel exactor, but a forgiver of the sins of the whole world. Wherefore, if thou be a sinner (as indeed are we all), set not Christ down upon the rainbow as a judge, but take hold of His true definition—namely, that Christ the Son of God and of the Virgin is a Person not that terrifieth, not that afflicteth, not that condemneth us of sin, not that demandeth an account of us for our life of evil passed, but hath given Himself for our sins, and with one oblation hath put away the sins of the whole world, hath fastened them upon the cross, and put them clean out by Himself.

CHRIST, then, is no Moses, no exactor, no giver of laws, but a giver of grace; a Saviour, and one that is full of mercy. Briefly, He is nothing else but infinite mercy and goodness, freely given, and bountifully giving unto us.

Now, as it is the greatest knowledge and cunning that Christians can have thus to define Christ, so of all things it is the hardest.

I speak not this without cause, for I know what moveth me to be so earnest that we should learn to define Christ out of the words of Paul.

Ye young men, therefore, are in this case much more happy than we that are old. For ye are not infected with these pernicious errors wherein I have been so nustled * and drowned from my youth, that at the very hearing of the name of Christ my heart hath trembled and quaked for fear.

Christ, when He cometh, is nothing else but joy and sweetness to a trembling, broken heart, as Paul here witnesseth, who setteth Him out with this most sweet and comfortable title when he saith, " *Which loved me and gave Himself for me.*" Christ, therefore, in very deed is a lover of those which are in trouble and anguish, in sin and death, and such a lover as gave Himself for us, who is also our High Priest.

He saith not, "Which hath *received* our works at our hands," nor "Which hath received the sacrifices of Moses' law, worshippings, religions, masses, vows and pilgrimages;" but hath "*given*." What? Not gold nor silver, nor beasts, nor paschal lambs, nor an angel, but Himself. For what? Not for a crown, not for a kingdom, not for our holiness and righteousness, but for our sins. Not for feigned or counterfeit sins, nor yet for small sins, nor for vanquished sins, but for great and huge sins; not for one or two, but for all.

Christ the Centre.

"IN my heart," he said, "this article reigns alone, and shall reign—namely, faith in

---

* Sixteenth century translation of the Commentary on the Galatians, probably the very same of which John Bunyan found the well-worn copy, which seemed "as if it had been written out of his heart."

my dear Lord Christ, who is the only Beginning, Middle, and End of all my spiritual and divine thoughts which I have by day or night."

Yet at the same time I feel that I only attain to a little feeble lifting up before others of the height, depth, and breadth, of this immeasurable and endless wisdom, and have scarcely been able to bring to light more than a few little fragments and broken pieces from this most rich and precious mine.

Christ the Priest.

ONCE, when his servant read in the Psalms the verse, "*I have sworn and will not repent, Thou art a Priest for ever,*" Doctor Martin said, "That is the most beautiful and glorious verse in the whole Psalter; for herein God holds forth this Christ alone as our Bishop and High Priest, who Himself and no other, without ceasing, makes intercession for His own with the Father. Not Caiaphas, nor Annas, nor Peter, nor Paul, nor the Pope; He, He alone shall be the Priest. This I affirm with an oath."

"*Thou art a Priest for ever.*" In that saying every syllable is greater than the whole Tower of Babel.

To this Priest let us cling and cleave. For He is faithful; He has given Himself for us to God, and holds us dearer than His own life.

When we stand firm to Christ, there is no other god in heaven or on earth but One who makes just and blessed. On the other hand, if we lose Him from our heart and eyes, there is no other help, comfort, or rest.

Christ our Sacrifice.

IN His death He is a Sacrifice, satisfying for our sins; in the resurrection, a Conqueror; in the ascension, a King; in the intercession, a High Priest.

Christ made One with Man.

GOD sent His only Son into the world, and laid upon Him the sins of all men, saying, "Be Thou Peter, that denier; Paul, that persecutor, blasphemer, and cruel oppressor; David, that adulterer; that sinner which did eat the apple in Paradise; that thief which hanged upon the cross; and briefly, be Thou the person which hath committed the sins of all men."

Christ Obedient to the Law.

CHRIST is not a Teacher of the law, like Moses, but a disciple who would be obedient to the law, that through such subjection and obedience He might redeem those who were under the law.

Christ Conquering by Suffering.

CHRIST is made the law of the law, the sin of sin, the death of death, that He might redeem from the curse of the law, justify me and quicken me. While He is the law, He is also liberty; while He is sin, He is righteousness; while He is death, He is life. For in that He suffered the law to accuse Him, sin to condemn Him, and death to devour Him, He abolished the law, He condemned sin, He destroyed death, He justified and saved me.

Christ our Life.

THIS life that I have now in the flesh, in very deed is no true life, but a shadow of life, under which another liveth; that is to say, Christ. Who is my true life, indeed; which life thou seest not, but only hearest, and I feel.

Christ Cleansing Us.

AS if He would say (in washing the disciples' feet), I am the true Laver and Bath. Therefore, if I wash thee not, thou remainest unclean, and dead in thy sins.

Christ the Conqueror of Sin, Death, and the Curse.

NOT only my sins and thine, but the sins of the whole world, either past, present, or to come, take hold of Him, go about to condemn Him, and do indeed condemn Him.

But because in the self-same Person—which

is thus the highest, the greatest, and the only sinner—there is also an everlasting and invincible righteousness, therefore these two do encounter together ; the highest, the greatest, and the only sin ; and the highest, the greatest, and the only righteousness.

Sin is a mighty and cruel tyrant, ruling and reigning over the whole world, bringing all men into bondage. This tyrant flieth upon Christ, and will needs swallow Him up, as he doth all other. But he seeth not that He is a person of invincible and everlasting righteousness. In this combat what is done ? Righteousness is everlasting, immortal, invincible.

In like manner, Death, which is an invincible queen and empress of the whole world, killing kings, princes, and, generally, all men, doth mightily encounter with Life, thinking utterly to overcome it ; and that which it undertaketh, it bringeth to pass indeed. But because Life was immortal, therefore, when it was overcome, yet did it truly overcome, and get the victory, vanquishing and killing death. Death, therefore, through Christ is vanquished and abolished throughout the whole world ; so that now it is but a painted death, which, losing its sting, can no more hurt those that believe in Christ, who is become the death of death.

So, the curse fighteth against the blessing, and would condemn it and bring it to naught ; but it cannot do so. For the blessing is divine, everlasting, and therefore the curse must needs give place. For if the blessing in Christ could be overcome, then should God Himself also be overcome.

The Name of Jesus.

IF God takes me this hour, or to-morrow, out of this life, I will leave it behind me, that I confess Jesus Christ to be my God and Lord. This I have learned, not from the Scriptures only, but in many great and hard experiences. I have resisted well-nigh unto blood, and endured many a sore conflict on this account ; but it has been very good and profitable for me.

The Gospel in the Crucifix.

I BELIEVE that many have been saved under the Papacy, although they never heard the gospel as now, thank God, it is preached and taught, to whom, as they were in the agony of death, and about to depart, the crucifix was held up, and it was said, " Fix thy hope on Him who hath redeemed thee."

II.

RULES OF THE SERVICE.

Obedience a Glorious Apparel.

HER *clothing is all glorious within.* What kind of glorious apparel is this? For we know that on earth Christians are poor and little esteemed. It is a spiritual adorning; not gold, silver, pearls, velvet, but obedience to the Lord our God. This apparel is brighter than the sun, for these are God's jewels. He who goes about doing God's will, goes about clothed in God's beauty. To serve Him truly, is simply to abide in our calling, be it lowly as it may.

WHEN one asked what was the best service of God, which pleased Him best? Doctor Martin said, "To hear Christ and be obedient to Him." This is the highest and greatest service of God. Besides this, all is worth nothing. For in heaven He has far better and more beautiful worship and service than we can render. As it was said to Saul, " *To obey is better than to sacrifice.*" As also soldiers say in time of war; obedience and keeping to the articles of war—this is victory.

EVEN in philosophy men are constrained not to look on the bare work, but on the goodwill of the worker. Wherefore we must ascend up higher in divinity with this word "doing" than in natural things and philosophy, so that now it must have a new signification, and be made altogether new.

TRUE obedience to God is the obedience of faith and good works; that is, he is truly obedient to God who trusts Him and does what He commands.

CHRISTIANS have to do with two kinds of business; the Word and the works of God.

IN all works we should look to God's Word. Such works as are done at God's command, these are not from our self-will; but we are God's tools and instruments, through which He works; they are not our own works, but God's. But all works which are not done at God's command are godless and condemned, being mere works of our own hands.

THE true doer of the law is he who, receiving the Holy Ghost through faith in Christ, beginneth to love God and to do good to his neighbor. The tree must be first, and then the fruit.

TO worship God in spirit, is the service and homage of the heart, and implies fear of God and trust in Him.

ALL Christians constitute the spiritual estate; and the only difference among them is that of the functions which they discharge.

The Law and the Gospel.

THE law discovers the disease. The gospel gives the remedy.

THE law is what we must do; the gospel what God will give.

THE gospel is like a fresh, soft, cool breeze in the great heat of summer, a comfort in anguish of conscience; not in winter, when there is already cold enough (that is in time of peace, when people are secure); but in the great heat of summer—that is, in those who truly feel terror and anguish of conscience, and God's anger against them.

THIS heat is caused by the sun. So must this terror of conscience be caused by the preaching of the law. Then must the heavenly breeze again quicken and refresh the conscience.

BUT when the powers are thus again quickened by the sweet wind of the gospel, we must not lie idly basking, we must show our faith by good works.

LIKE as the parched earth coveteth the rain, the law maketh parched and troubled souls to thirst after Christ.

THE law is a light which enlightens us not to see God's grace nor righteousness, through which we attain to eternal life, but sin, our infirmities, death, God's anger, and judgment.

THE gospel is a far different light. It lights up the troubled heart, makes it live again, comforts and helps. For it shows how God forgives unworthy, condemned sinners for Christ's sake, when they believe that they are redeemed by His death; and that through His victory are given to them all blessings, grace, forgiveness of sins, righteousness, and eternal life.

The Law a Fire.

THE law is that hammer, that fire, that mighty and strong wind, and that terrible earthquake, rending the mountains and shivering the rocks. But it behooved that the tempest, the fire, the wind, the earthquake, should pass, before the Lord should reveal Himself in the still small voice.

The Law a Prison.

THE law is a prison, both civilly and spiritually. For, first, it restraineth and shutteth up the wicked; furthermore, by revealing sin, it shutteth man up in a prison, out of which he cannot escape.

The Law a Schoolmaster.

THE law is not barely a schoolmaster, but a schoolmaster to bring us to Christ. For what a schoolmaster were he which should alway torment and beat the child, and teach him nothing at all? And yet such schoolmasters there were in times past, when schools were nothing else but a prison and a very hell; the schoolmasters cruel tyrants and very butchers; the children were always beaten; they learned with continual pain and travail, and yet few of them came to any proof. The law is not such a schoolmaster. For it doth not only terrify and torment. It instructeth, and exerciseth, and with its rods driveth us to Christ.

"IF Moses comes to judge me," said Doctor Martin, "I will motion him away, in God's name, and say, 'Here stands Christ.' And at the Last Day, Moses will look on me and say, 'Thou hast understood me aright.' And he will be gracious to me."

The Law a Wall of Defence.

BY the Ten Commandments the Lord hath defended and fortified the life of man, his wife and children, and his goods, as it were with a wall, against the force and violence of the wicked.

The Decalogue to be taught Affirmatively.

THE Decalogue (that, is the Ten Commandments of God) is a mirror and brief summary of all virtues, and teaches how we should conduct ourselves towards God and towards man. And no more beautiful, perfect, and shorter book of virtues was ever written.

The virtue of the First Commandment is godliness; that is, to fear, love, and trust God.

Of the Second, to confess and preach the doctrine of God's word.

Of the Third, public worship of God.

Of the Fourth, obedience to parents, preceptors, and rulers in that which is not contrary to God.

Of the Fifth, gentleness, not to be revengeful.
Of the Sixth, chastity and sobriety.
Of the Seventh, to do good, willingly give and lend, and be generous.
Of the Eighth, truth, to injure no one's good name, to speak good of each other.
Of the Ninth, justice, to let each enjoy his own.
Of the Tenth, to be without evil desires in the heart, and to be content with our own.

The Ten Commandments are to be understood and explained as not only forbidding, but bidding. "The chief commandment is love from a pure heart, and a good conscience, and faith unfeigned."

THAT word, "*Thou shalt have none other Gods but Me,*" once seemed to me useless and superfluous under the gospel. When I read it first, I thought, " Ah, who does not know that ? " But now, thank God, I see what the words mean ; indeed, they are more wonderful than any man can explain or comprehend.

Short Sayings about the Catechism as Dr. Martin Luther taught it at Home.

THE COMMANDMENTS.

AS faith is, so is God.

God does not remain outside, although He delays.

Idolatry is essentially darkness of heart.
God gives through creatures.
Unthankfulness is theft
No one should be judged in his absence.
Interpret all for the best.
No good work goes beyond the Ten Commandments.
To fear and trust God is fulfilling all the Commandments.
The First Commandment includes all the rest.

THE CREED.

GOD gives Himself to us with all the creatures.
The Holy Spirit brings Christ home to us.
Where the Holy Spirit does not preach, there is no church.
The work of the Holy Spirit is going forward perpetually.

GOOD WORKS.

THE good works of Christians are to benefit and help our neighbors.
In tribulations we should be manly and of a good heart.
Our whole life should be manly, fearing and trusting God.
Faith makes us the inheritance of Christ.
The gospel is pure joy.
The person must be good before his works.

A Christian life consists in three things—in faith, love, and the cross.*

A clergyman is like the director of a hospital.

God's gifts which we possess, we should esteem highly; ourselves humbly.

THE Decalogue is a doctrine beyond all doctrines. The Apostles' Creed is virtue beyond all virtues. The Lord's Prayer is a prayer beyond all prayers and Litanies; moreover, it is a joy above all joys. For as the Ten Commandments teach and exhort all in the freest and fullest way, so the Creed fulfils the same in the most thorough way, and the Lord's Prayer asks and entreats all in the most Christian and certain way. Therefore this threefold cord makes a man perfect in thought, speech, and work, ordering and educating his heart, mind, tongue, and body to the highest perfection.

The Decalogue based on Redemption.

THUS saith God, "*I am the Lord thy God, who led thee out of the land of Egypt.*" Because God can only be known through His acts and works. He points us to a glorious act whereby we may know what a God we honor and serve—namely, the God who delivered Israel

---

* Elsewhere he says, "Faith, confession, and the cross make a true Christian."

from the house of bondage; the God who has given us His Word, and His Son Christ, who has suffered and died for us; the God who awakened Him again from the dead.

Fulfilling the Duties of our Calling the best Service of God.

ST. PAUL in his Epistles has written more fully and wisely of virtues and good works than all the philosophers, for he exalts and gloriously commends the works of each man's calling.

HE said, "Master Joachim Mörlein has pleased me well to-day with his sermon, for he spoke of the office and vocation of a wife, and a maid-servant—namely, that a wife should think she lives in a Holy Order, and that a servant also may know that her works are good and holy works. This the people can carry home."

IF a peasant knew the perils and toils of a prince, he would thank God that he was a peasant, and in the happiest and safest state. But the peasants know not their happiness and welfare. They look only on the outside pomp of princes, their fine clothes, golden chains, great castles, and houses; but see not the care and peril wherein princes live, as in a fire and a deluge.

PEASANTS' work is among the happiest, for it is full of hope. Ploughing, sowing, planting, propping, pruning, mowing, threshing, wood-cutting, are all labors full of hope.

SO, also, men and maidens in a house are often better off than their masters and mistresses, for they have no household cares—have only to do their work, and when this is done, it is done; and they can eat, and drink, and sing. My Wolf, and Orthe (Dorothea), my man, and my cook, are better off than my Kâttie or I, for married life and the ordering of a household bring with them their trials and the holy cross.

HE spoke of the legends of the holy Patriarchs, how far they exceeded the holiness of (reputed) saints, because they simply went on their way, in obedience to God, in the works of their calling, and did what came to their hand to do, according to God's commandment, without choosing for themselves.

Two Vocations, of Faith and of Love.

NO one can understand any work aright unless he is called to it.

Vocation is of two kinds. Either it is divine, comes from above, or from those who have the right to command; and then it is a Vocation of Faith.

Or it is a Vocation of Love, and comes from our equals.

Two Sacrifices.

THE first was called in the Old Testament the early or morning sacrifice. By this it was shadowed forth that we should first sacrifice to God, not calves and oxen, but *ourselves*, acknowledging God's gifts, both bodily and spiritual, temporal and eternal, and giving Him thanks.

The second the evening sacrifice. By this it was signified that a Christian should offer to God a broken, lowly, contrite heart, which confesses both its sin and danger, bodily and spiritual, and cries to God for help.

What Obedience meant to Luther.

AT THE DIET OF WORMS.

"HERE I stand: I can do no otherwise. God help me. Amen."

AT AUGSBURG.

"THREE whole days I was at Augsburg, without the Imperial safe-conduct. Meantime they earnestly entreated me to say 'Revoco.'

"After three days the Bishop of Trent came and showed me the safe-conduct. Then I went in all humility to the Cardinal; fell at first on my knee; the second time on the ground; the third time prostrate there so long that three times he bid me rise. Then I arose. That pleased him much. He hoped I would think better of it.

"When I came to the Cardinal the second time, and would not recant, he said:

"'What meanest thou? Dost think the princes will defend thee with arms and armies? Surely, no! Where, then, wilt thou take refuge?'

"I said, 'Under heaven.'"

DURING THE PLAGUE AT WITTENBURG.

"IF the lot fell on me, I would not shrink from the plague. I have been with many when they had it. I have now remained through three pestilences without fleeing."

Merit.

MERIT is a work for the sake of which Christ gives rewards. But no such work is to be found, for Christ gives by promise. Just as if a prince were to say to me: "Come to me in my castle, and I will give you a hundred florins." I do a work, certainly, in going to the castle, but the gift is not given me as the reward of my work in going, but because the prince promised it me.

III.

THE WEAPONS OF OUR WARFARE.

Faith.

FAITH is nothing else but the truth of the heart; that is to say, a true and right opinion of the heart as touching God.

FAITH is the divinity of works, and is so spread throughout the works of the faithful as is the divinity throughout the humanity of Christ.

Through faith we do good works. Through good works faith is made visible and comprehensible. As the Godhead cannot be seen nor comprehended, but when Christ became incarnate He was seen and handled.

In all our doings, spiritual and bodily, faith must rule and reign, and the heart hold it sure and firm, that God is looking on us, holds us dear, will help us, and not forsake us.

CHRISTIAN faith is not an idle quality or empty husk in the heart, until charity come and quicken it, but if it be true faith, it is a sure trust and confidence in the heart, and a firm consent whereby Christ is apprehended, so that Christ is the object of faith, yea, rather, even in faith Christ himself is present.

Faith, therefore, is a certain obscure knowledge, or rather darkness which seeth nothing, and yet Christ apprehended by faith sitteth in the darkness.

The school divines do dream that faith is a quality cleaving in the heart, without Christ. But Christ should be so set forth that thou shouldst see nothing besides him, and shouldst think that nothing can be more unto thee, or more present with thy heart than He is. For he sitteth not idly in Heaven, but is present with us, working and living in us.

Faith, therefore, is a certain steadfast beholding, which looketh upon nothing else but Christ, the conqueror of sin and death, and the giver of righteousness, salvation, and eternal life.

FOR he that is a Christian hath Christ the Lord of the law present and enclosed in his heart, even as a ring hath a jewel or precious stone enclosed in it.

He that hath faith in the heart hath such a treasure, that though it seemeth to be but little, is greater than heaven and earth, because Christ "the unspeakable gift" is greater.

THE believing man hath the Holy Ghost, and where the Holy Ghost dwelleth, He will not suffer a man to be idle, but stirreth him up to all exercises of piety and godliness, and of true religion, to the love of God, to the patient suffering of afflictions to prayer, to thanksgiving, and to the exercise of charity towards all men.

BECAUSE thou hast laid hold on Christ by faith, through whom thou art made righteousness, begin now to work well. Love God and thy neighbor, call upon God, praise Him, and confess Him. These are good works indeed, which flow out of this faith and this cheerfulness conceived in the heart, for that we have remission of sins freely by Christ.

The Reflex Action of Faith.
THE FORCE OF PRONOUNS.

BUT weigh diligently every word of Paul, and especially mark well this pronoun "*our ;*" for the effect altogether consisteth in the well-applying of pronouns, which we find very often in the Scriptures; wherein also there is ever some vehemency and power.

Therefore, generally, it is an easy matter to magnify and amplify the benefit of Christ, namely that Christ was given for sins, but for other men's sins, which are worthy. But when it cometh to the putting to of this pronoun "*our*," there our weak nature and reason starteth back, and dare not come nigh unto God, nor promise to herself that so great a treasure shall be freely given unto her.

WHEREFORE these words, "*Which loveth Me*," are full of faith. And he who can utter this word "*me*," and apply it unto himself with a true and constant faith as Paul did, shall be a good disputer with Paul against the law.

For He delivered neither sheep, ox, gold nor silver, but even God Himself entirely and wholly "for me," even "*for me*," I say, a miserable and wretched sinner.

HUMAN wit treats these words, "*Who gave Himself for our sins*," as if the sins were not real, true sins; as if the words were said lightly, and not, as they are, in true, bitter earnest.

Faith Lifting us to God's Horizon.

PSALM XXXVII. "*For they shall soon be cut down like the grass.*" He lifts us from our horizon to God's. In our sight the wicked flourish and increase and cover the whole earth. But in God's sight what are they? Hay! The higher the grass is, the nearer the hay-fork.

PSALM XXIII. "*But the Lord shall laugh at him, for He seeth that his day cometh.*"

Not that God laughs, like a man; but that in truth it is a laughable thing to see foolish men raging (against the truth), and undertaking great things which they cannot really advance one hair's breadth.

Just as a fool would be ridiculous, who with a long spear and a short dagger were to seek to smite the Sun out of the heavens, and with this prospect were to shout and glorify himself as if he had accomplished a grand feat.

Faith and Hope.

FAITH is a teacher and a judge, fighting against errors and heresies, judging spirits and doctrines.

But Hope is, as it were, the general and captain of the field, fighting against temptation, the cross, impatience, heaviness of spirit, desperation and blaspheming, and it waiteth for good things, even in the midst of all evils.

FAITH and hope are in many ways distinguished. Faith is in the understanding of man; hope in the will; and yet these two can no more be severed than the cherubim above the mercy seat.

According to their offices; faith dictates, distinguishes, teaches, and is knowledge and science.

But hope exhorts, awakens, listens, waits, and patiently endures.

Faith looks to the word and the promise, that is, the truth. But hope looks to that which the Word has promised, to the gifts.

Faith exists at the beginning of life, before all tribulations and adversities. But hope follows afterwards and grows out of adversities.

Faith strives against error and heresy. But hope strives against tribulation and temptation.

As foresight and understanding are useless, and effect nothing without manhood and cheerfulness, so is faith nothing without hope; for hope endures and overcomes misfortune and evil. And as a joyful heart without foresight and understanding is foolhardiness, so is hope without faith.

Faith and hope are thus distinguished. Faith says, I believe in a resurrection of the dead at the Last Day. To this hope adds, "Then, if this is true, let us give up what we have, and suffer what we can, if hereafter we are to be such great princes."

ALL which happens in the whole world happens through hope. No husbandman would sow a grain of corn, if he did not hope it would spring up and bring forth the ear. How much more are we helped on by hope in the way to eternal life.

Faith and Charity.

CHARITY giveth place, for it "suffereth all things." But faith giveth no place; yea, it can suffer nothing. As concerning faith, we ought to be invincible and more hard, if it might be, than the adamant stone. But as touching charity we ought to be soft, and more flexible than the reed or leaf that is shaken by the wind, and ready to yield to everything.

SEE the sun! It brings us two things—light and heat. The rays of light beam directly on us. No king is powerful enough to intercept those keen, direct and swift rays. But heat is radiated back to us from every side. Thus, like the light, faith should ever be direct and inflexible; but love, like the heat, should radiate on all sides, and meekly adapt itself to the wants of all

The Trial of Faith.

THE trial of faith is the greatest and heaviest of all trials. For faith it is which must conquer in all trials. Therefore, if faith gives way, then the smallest and most trifling temptations can overcome a man. But when faith is sound and true, then all other temptations must yield, and be overcome.

"ALAS! that we believe God so little," he said. "I can trust my wife, and all of you, my friends, more than I can trust Him. Yet none of you would do and suffer for me what He did; would suffer yourselves to be crucified for me."

SECURE, easy spirits, like all false Christians, when they have glanced over the Bible and heard a few sermons, soon persuade themselves they have the Holy Ghost, and that they understand and know all things.

Ah! true hearts find it far otherwise; these pray every day, yea, every moment: "Lord, strengthen our faith."

REAL believers are always thinking they believe not, therefore they are fighting, wrestling, striving, and toiling without ceasing, to preserve and increase their faith. Just as good and skilful masters of any art are always seeing and observing that something is lacking in their work, whilst bunglers and pretenders persuade themselves that they lack nothing, but that all they make and do is quite perfect.

OUR faith is weak, and yet it is a rock; for it is the corner-stone of the heart.

Martin Luther's own Faith in Trial.
Letter from Coburg, during the Diet of Augsburg.
To the Elector Frederic, of Saxony.

AS to my affairs, my gracious lord, I answer thus: Your Electoral Grace knows (or if your Electoral Grace does not know, I hereby make it known), I have not received the Gospel from man, but from heaven, only through our Lord Jesus Christ, so that I might well esteem and subscribe myself (as henceforth I will) His servant and evangelist. That I have at any time submitted myself to human hearing and judgment was not because I doubted this, but from humility, to win others.

Now, however, that I see how my too great humility will lead to the degrading of the Gospel, and that if I yield the devil a hand's breadth, he will take the whole place, by constraint of my conscience I must act otherwise. I have yielded enough this year, in deference to your Electoral Grace; for the devil knows well it was no faint-heartedness that made me yield. He saw my heart well, when I came into Worms; that if I had known that as many devils would set upon me as there are tiles on the roofs, I would have leapt down among them with joy.

After all, Duke George is far from being equal to one single devil. And since the Father of unfathomable mercy has, through the Gospel, made us joyful lords over all the devils, and over death, and has given us such wealth of trust that we can say to Him, "most dear Father," it would indeed be the most shameful slight to such a Father that we could not trust Him to make us lords over Duke George's wrath.

This, at least, I know well of myself; if needful I would ride into Leipzig, if it rained Duke Georges nine days, and each Duke George were ninefold more furious than this one.

They hold my Lord Christ to be a man twisted of straw! This may my Lord, and I, for a while, indeed, endure.

It is another than Duke George with whom I have to do, who knows me pretty well, and I know Him not ill.

Your Electoral Grace is only lord over goods and bodies. But Christ is Lord also over souls, to whom He has sent me, and to that end has awakened me. These souls I dare not forsake. I hope my Lord Christ will overcome our foes, and will be well able to shield me from them, if He so will. If so he will not, His dear will be done.

Letter to Melanchthon during the Diet of Augsburg.

THE end and event of the cause troubles thee, that thou canst not order it. But if thou couldst comprehend it, then would I be no partaker in such a cause, much less the author of it.

God has placed this cause in a certain common place, which thou hast not in thy rhetoric, nor in thy philosophy. It is called Faith, in which place are set all things invisible, and that do not appear, which things, if any one seeks to render visible, apparent and comprehensible, as thou art doing, he shall reap cares and tears as the reward of his labor, which in truth thou art reaping, all of us meanwhile warning thee in vain.

God dwelleth in the clouds, and has set this darkness as His curtain. Let him who will, change this.

If Moses had insisted on knowing the end, and how he was to escape the hosts of Pharaoh, Israel would probably have been in Egypt to this day.

To Brentius on Melanchthon's Fears.

AFTER us, God will be the Creator, as He was before us, and is to-day, with us. He will not die with us, nor cease to be God, ruling even men's thoughts.

It seemed to Eli, the priest, that the kingdom of Israel was perishing, the ark being taken by the Philistines; but Eli perished first, and the kingdom afterwards began to flourish most.

Philip designs to be head-ruler of the world, that is to crucify himself. But I know that He will be, in the future, who said, "*Where is Abel, thy brother?*"

If God exists, not here only do we live; but wherever He lives we shall live. If these things are true, what, I ask, are these furious threats of idols, not merely dying, but wholly lifeless? He who created me will be the Father of my son, a Husband to my wife, the Ruler of my country, the Preacher to my parish, and better than all that (when I am gone).

To Shalatin.

PHILIP thinks to accomplish his own counsel. *Sic fecissem ego.* No! it must not be "*Sic ego Philippus.*" The "*ego*" is too small. The word is, "*I am that I am.*"

Do thou exhort Philip in my name not to make himself God, but to fight against that innate ambition of divinity implanted in us by the Devil in Paradise. This cast Adam out of Paradise, and this only disquiets us, and casts us out of peace.

We are to be men, and not God. This is the sum of the whole matter. Otherwise eternal unrest and heart-sorrow is our portion.

To Justus Jonas.

CHRIST has come; and He sitteth at the right hand, not of Cæsar, but of God, This may be very incredible. I nevertheless delight in this incredible thing; and therein I will dare to die. Why, then, should I not live therein?

I would that Philip would take this my faith, if he has none beside.

"On the right hand," is indeed a little thing; but the "*My*," "My right hand;" where has that an end?

The pronoun does it. The name Adonai, which follows the "*I have said*," will take good care of the precious "*Sit Thou*," until "*Thy foes Thy footstool*" shall also come. What recks it, if David falls?

Farewell in Christ, and believe us, as thou dost, that Christ is King of kings and Lord of lords. If He lose this title at Augsburg, He will have lost it in heaven and on earth. Amen.

To the Chancellor Brück, at Augsburg, from " the Wilderness" (Coburg).

TWO MIRACLES.

I HAVE lately seen two miracles. The first, as I was looking out of the window, and saw the stars in heaven, and the whole fair vault of God, yet saw nowhere any pillars whereon the Master had raised this vault. Nevertheless the heavens fell not, and that fair vault stands firm.

Now, there are some who search for the pillars, and would fain grasp and feel them. And because they cannot do this they totter and tremble as if the heavens must surely fall, from no other cause save that they cannot grasp these pillars, nor see them. If they could grasp these pillars, then (no doubt) the heavens would stand firm!

The second miracle is this. I saw also vast, thick clouds lowering over us, with such a weight that they might be compared to a great ocean. Yet saw I no floor whereon they were based, nor any shore whereby they were bound. Nevertheless they fell not on us, but saluted us with a frowning countenance and fled away.

When they had passed by, then shone forth their floor, whereon they were based, and also our roof, the rainbow. Yet that was indeed a feeble, slight, insignificant floor and roof; so slight that it faded away into the clouds, and was more like a prism, such as is wont to stream through painted glass, than such a mighty floor; so that one might well have despaired on account of the feebleness of the floor, as much as on account of the great weight of the waters.

Nevertheless it was found, in fact, that this feeble prism bore up the weight of waters and shielded us.

Yet there are some who look at the mass and weight of the clouds, and consider these more than this slight, subtile, narrow prism. They would fain feel the power of the prism, and because they cannot do this, they fear that the clouds will pour down an eternal deluge.

The Sea Restrained by a Rope of Sand.

LET the adversaries rage and storm as long as they can. God has set its bound to the sea. He suffers it to rage and swell, and to rush on with its waves in vehement assaults, as if it would cover and overwhelm all things. But nevertheless it does not pass the shore, although God binds it not with bands of iron, but of sand.

THROUGH what inner conflict this faith of Luther's was maintained, I have and know nothing of Jesus Christ (since I have not seen him with my bodily eyes, nor heard with my bodily ears), save only His name. Yet have I, thank God, learned so much of Him from the Scriptures that I am well contented therewith, and desire not to see or hear Him in the flesh. Moreover, in my deepest weakness, in terrors and pressure of the burden of sin, in fear and trembling before death, in persecution from the false, cruel world, often have I experienced and felt the divine power of this name in me, abandoned as I was by all creatures. I have proved its power to snatch me from death, to make me live again, to comfort me in the greatest despair, especially during the Diet of Augsburg in the year 1530.

Prayer.

AS a shoemaker makes shoes, and a tailor coats, so should a Christian pray. *Prayer* is the Christian's business. Let us pray and strive; for the word of faith and the prayer of the just are the mightiest weapons.

A COMPLAINT was once made to Doctor Martin Luther, "Dear Herr Doctor, things are issuing and happening nowhere as we would have them." "Well," he said, "that is precisely right. Have you not given up your will to our Lord God, praying every day, *Thy will be done on earth as it is in heaven?*"

OH, it is a great and mighty thing, the prayer of the just. But God knows best how and when to grant our prayers, for if He did always as we would, He would be our captive. I prayed once for the life of a suffering woman, with great anguish and wrestling of heart. But God knew best. He did indeed hear our prayer in such a way that in the life to come that good woman will thank me for it.

WE should commit all to God. He will make it all well. "*Even to hoar hairs I will carry you; I have made, and I will bear. I will carry and deliver you.* Therefore lay it all on me, my beloved; commit it to me."

So Saint Peter: "*Casting all your care upon Him.*" That is a choice, consoling saying. And "*Cast thy burden on the Lord, and He will sustain thee.*"

Ah, these are beautiful, comforting sayings! But we want to do and order all ourselves, although we are not able, yea it is impossible.

We want to lift and carry all ourselves, and forget our Lord God, and so we sink, and make the evil worse.

Indeed, sayest thou, I have committed all to Him, but He will not come, He delays too long. Oh, wait on the Lord—we must wait and hold on; for at last he will surely come.

ALL who call on God in true faith, earnestly, from the heart, will certainly be heard, and will receive what they have asked and desired, although not in the hour or in the measure, or the very thing which they ask; yet they will obtain something greater and more glorious than they had dared to ask.

THE cry and sigh of the heart raises a clamor that not only God but all the angels in heaven must hear. Thus, Moses was dismayed when he came to the Red Sea. He cried with trembling, shuddering, and dismay, and nevertheless did not open his mouth. "O Lord God," he said, "what shall I do now? How can I find my way out? I am the cause that all this people will be here miserably murdered. There is no help nor counsel. Before us is the sea; behind us are our foes, the Egyptians; on both sides high mountains. It is all over with us." Then God answered, "Wherefore criest thou unto me."
—*Exodus xiv.* 13, 14, 15.

But we read their examples as if they were a dead letter.

Moses must have heaved a great sigh, that he filled therewith the ears of God. It is contrary to all which reason could have expected that they went through the Red Sea. For their way through the Red Sea is as broad as from Wittenburg to Coburg, or at least from Wittenburg to Magdeburg. In the night, moreover, they must have rested and eaten. For six hundred thousand men, not including women and children, even if they went three hundred and fifty, or even five hundred abreast, must have taken time.

Thus the cry of Moses seemed to Moses indeed little, but to God great.

WE think this groaning which we make in these terrors, and this weakness, scarcely to be a groaning, far less a cry. For our faith, which in temptation thus groaneth unto Christ, is very weak if we consider our own sense and feeling, and therefore we hear not this cry.

But to the searcher of hearts this small and feeble groaning (as it seemeth unto us), is a loud and mighty cry, in comparison whereof the great and horrible roarings of the law, of sin, of death, of the devil, and of hell, are as nothing, neither can they even be heard. It filleth heaven, so that the angels think they hear nothing but this cry.

These feeble cries were our guns and artillery wherewith we have, so many years, scattered the counsels and enterprises of our adversaries.

NO one believes how mighty and strong prayer is, and how much it can do, save he who has learned by experience and tried it. But it is a great thing, when any one feels great need pressing on him, if he can grasp prayer.

FOR I know, as often as I have earnestly prayed, when it has been real earnest with me I have indeed been richly heard, and have obtained more than I have prayed for. God has for a time delayed, but nevertheless the help has come.

Ah, how truly grand a thing is the honest prayer of a true Christian! How mighty it is with God; that a poor human creature can so speak with the High Majesty in Heaven, and not dread him, but know that God is kindly smiling on him, for Jesus Christ's sake, His dear Son, our Lord and Saviour! To this end, the heart and conscience must not look back, must not doubt or fear on account of unworthiness.

THE ancients have well described prayer as the lifting up of the heart to God. It was well said. But I and many others in olden times did not understand the definition aright. We spoke and boasted of "the lifting up of the heart," the "*ascensus mentis;*" but our syntax failed, for we could not add the "*Deum*," the word God.

DEAR brethren, pray with the heart, sometimes also with the lips; for prayer sustains the world: without prayer things would be far otherwise.

THE prayer of the Church works great miracles. In our own days it has raised three from the dead; myself, who have often lain sick to death; my wife Käthe, who was also sick to death; and Philip Melanchthon, who, in 1540, lay sick to death at Weimar.

Yet these are poor miracles, to be observed on account of those who are weak in faith.

Far greater miracles to me are these: that our Lord God every day in the Church baptizes, gives the Sacrament of the Altar, absolves, and delivers from sin, from death, and eternal damnation. These are to me the great miracles.

What a strong wall and fortification to the Church, and what a weapon for Christians is prayer!

Ah, what an excellent Master composed the Lord's Prayer! What an endless rhetoric and eloquence lies hidden in those words, wherein all things, all necessities, are comprehended.

The first three petitions embrace such great, excellent, and heavenly things, that no heart can ever fathom them.

The fourth petition gathers together all policy and economy, national and domestic government, and all which is bodily and temporal, and needful for this life.

The fifth contends against the devil of a bad conscience; against inborn and actual sins, which burden the conscience.

Truly One who is wise made this prayer, whom no man can rival.

AH, we have cried and prayed so long, and Thou wilt not give us rain! Surely, if Thou givest not rain, Thou wilt give something better—a still and quiet life.

THE prayer of the heart, and the complaints of the poor, raise such a cry that all the angels in heaven must hear it. Our Lord God hears, with quick, delicate hearing, the faintest breath.

THOSE deep sighs, in deep necessities, are the true great clamor and fervent cry before which the heavens are rent.

THE *causa efficiens* of prayer is simply faith itself. *Causa per accidens*, which drives us to prayer, is necessity. The *forma*, is to grasp the mercy so freely given. *Materia circa quam* is the promise, and the command of God to pray, to which prayer holds and cleaves, and on which it is based. *Finis* is the hearing and deliverance.

I have not yet prayed the whole Psalter through. The Lord's Prayer is my prayer.

GOD gives not according to the measure, manner, and time that we would prescribe. He will be unfettered. But He gives good measure, pressed down and running over, as Christ says.

Thus did St. Augustine's mother. She asked that her son might be converted. But it came not to pass. She went to all the learned men, that they might persuade him. At last she entreated him to marry a Christian maiden, that she might bring him to the faith. But nothing succeeded.

But when at last our Lord God comes, He comes indeed, and makes such an Augustine of him, that to this day he is called a light of the Church.

SOME have vehemently prayed for temptation, that they might not grow careless without the cross. I, however, will never more pray for temptation, but only, "Lead me not into temptation."

EVERY sigh of a Christian is a prayer; when he sighs he prays.

THIS saying, "Ask, and ye shall receive," means nothing less than ask, call, cry, knock, knock vehemently. And this we must do, on and on, without ceasing.

Intercession for those in Authority.

PRINCES and lords are poor people, especially when they are good and God-fearing; therefore our Lord God has not vainly commanded us to honor and pray for them.

I did not so well understand this command until I learned it with reference to my two Electors and lords, Duke John and Duke John Frederic. Often they cannot help if they would. Therefore they sorely need the prayer of Christians.

Praying and Waiting.

LET us pray and call on God in all tribulations, and wait.

Let us keep to Christ, and cling to Him, and hang on Him, so that no power can sever us. Then soon we shall see Him with joy, at that Day.

Thanksgiving.

THANKSGIVING makes our prayers bold and strong, easy, moreover, pleasant and sweet; feeds and enkindles them as with coals of fire.

Intercession.

CHRIST suffers not that one should pray for himself alone, but for the whole community of all men. For He teaches us not to say "My Father," but "Our Father." Prayer is a spiritual, common possession; therefore we must despoil no one of it, not even our enemies. For as He is the Father of us all, He wills that we shall be brothers amongst each other, and pray for one another, as for ourselves.

Prayer of Luther, Overheard during the Diet of Worms.

ALMIGHTY, everlasting God, how terrible this world is! How it would open its jaws to devour me. And how weak is my trust in Thee! The flesh is weak, and the devil is strong! O Thou my God, help me against all the wisdom of this world. Do Thou the work. It is for Thee alone to do it; for the work is Thine, not mine. I have nothing to bring me here. I have no controversy to maintain—not I—with the great ones of the earth. I, too, would fain that my days should glide along, happy and calm. But the cause is Thine. It is righteous; it is eternal. O Lord, help me! Thou that art faithful, Thou that art unchangeable! It is not in any man I trust. That were vain indeed. All that is in man gives way; all that comes from man faileth. O God, my God, dost Thou not hear me? Art Thou dead? No; Thou canst not die. Thou art hiding Thyself.

Thou hast chosen me for this work. I know it. Oh, then, arise and work! Be Thou on my side, for the sake of Thy beloved Son, Jesus

Christ, who is my defence, my shield, and my fortress.

O Lord my God, where art Thou? Come; come! I am ready—ready to forsake life for Thy truth; patient as a lamb. For it is a righteous cause, and it is Thine own. I will not depart from Thee now, nor through eternity. And although the world should be full of demons; although my body (which, nevertheless, is the work of Thy hands) should be doomed to bite the dust, to be stretched on the rack, cut into pieces, consumed to ashes, the soul is Thine. Yes; for this I have the assurance of Thy Word. My soul is Thine. It will abide near Thee throughout the endless ages. Amen. O God, help Thou me! Amen.

Amen, amen—that means *Yes, yes; that shall be done.*

The Word of God.

THE Word of God is a fiery shield, for this reason, that it is more enduring and purer than gold tried in the fire; which gold loses nothing in the fire, but it stands the fire, endures, and overcomes all trial. So, he who believes in the Word of God, overcomes all, and continues eternally secure against all misfortune. This shield shrinks not from the gates of hell, but the gates of hell tremble before it.

THE words of the Lord Christ are the most powerful; they have hands and feet, and overcome all attacks, all subtilties and devices of the wise. Thus we see in the Gospel how Christ, with quite simple, common words, brought to shame the wisdom of the Pharisees, so that they could find no escape from them.

It is a very acute and conclusive syllogism, when the Lord says, "*Render unto Cæsar the things that are Cæsar's:*" for He neither bids nor forbids to pay the tribute, but answers them with their own arguments; as if He had said, "If, indeed, you have suffered Cæsar to make such inroads that you have, and use his coinage, then give him what you owe him."

THERE is no greater grace or possession than to believe that God speaks to us. If we believed that, we should be already blessed.

Commentaries.

THROUGH so many commentaries and books the dear Bible is buried, so that people do not look at the text itself. It is far better to see with our own eyes than with other people's eyes. For which reason I could wish that all my own books were buried nine ells deep in the earth, on account of the bad example they may give to others to follow me in writing multitudes of books.

The Second Psalm.

THIS is a right lofty psalm against the enemies of God. It begins softly and simply, but it goes out with magnificence. It is a lofty, noble psalm. It says, Come and see what the Lord doeth. He has been now six thousand years in the Council, ruling and making all laws. *Habitator cœli.* He that dwelleth in the heavens takes our cause in hand.

MANY foes, Egyptian, Babylonian, Persian, Greek, and Roman, have raged against the Bible, endeavoring to extirpate it; but they have been able to accomplish nothing. They are all gone, but the book remains for ever perfect. Who then has preserved it, and defended it with such great power? No one surely but God Himself, who is the Master. And it is a great miracle that God has preserved the book so long, for the devil and the world hate it bitterly.

THE resurrection of the Lord Christ through the Word does not take place without an earthquake, as Christ Himself also did not come forth from the grave without an earthquake.

But such an earthquake is pleasanter to true hearts, than that Christ should lie in the grave and rest. When there is peace and rest in Christendom it is a bad sign.

WHEN the devil finds me idle and unarmed, not heeding God's Word, he works on my conscience that I have taught wrong, and stirred up by my doctrine much offence and division compared with the former state of the Church, which was still and peaceful.

I cannot deny I am often in depression and anguish on this account; but when I grasp the Word of God, I have won the battle.

WE see, and experience teaches us, how powerful and strong Divine Truth is; it presses through all the obstacles by which it is hemmed in; the more we read it, the more it moves us; it takes the heart captive, and creates other good thoughts.

The Sacraments.

Holy Baptism.

DOCTOR MARTIN LUTHER asked Doctor Hieronymus Weller "How it went with him?" "Sadly and mournfully," said he; "I know not how it is." Whereon Dr. Martin Luther replied, "Have you, then, not been baptized?" What a great gift of God is baptism! What a great gift also is the Word of God; we should thank God from our hearts that we have His Word. For it is God who comforts and strengthens us, and who has given us His Holy Spirit for a pledge and a foretaste.

HEAVEN is given to me freely, and is my (royal) gift, and I have letters and seals for it; that is, I am baptized and go to the sacrament. Therefore I take care of the letter, that the devil may not tear it in pieces; that is, I live and abide in the fear of God, and pray the Lord's Prayer.

God could not have given me salvation and the gospel save through the death, the suffering, and dying of His dear Son. And when I believe that He has overcome death, and has died for me, and I look at the promise of the Father, then I have the letter complete, and the seal of baptism and of the sacrament of the altar (the true essential body and blood of our Lord Christ) affixed to it; thus I am well provided for.

We should hold it certain that baptism is God's ordinance, which He has appointed, that we may know where we may surely find Him. He seeks us; He comes to us; we cannot come to Him of ourselves.

The Sacrament of the Altar.

"THE true cause of this sacrament," said Dr. Martin Luther, "is the word and appointment of Christ, who has instituted and established it. The *materia* is bread and wine; the *form* is the true body and blood of Christ; the *final cause* whereto it is ordained is the *use* and fruit, that we may strengthen our faith, and not doubt that the body of Christ is given for us, and His blood poured out for us, and that our sins are surely forgiven us through the death of Christ."

THIS sacrament can only be received and embraced by the heart; for it is not with the hand that we receive such a gift and eternal treasure.

THIS benefit and grace have we now received, that Christ is our Saviour, not our severe Judge; our Redeemer and Deliverer, not our accuser and jailer who takes us captive. For we are all sinners in Adam, guilty of eternal death, and condemned; but we are all now justified, redeemed, and consecrated by the blood of Christ. Let us grasp this with faith.

The Vow of Baptism the True and Highest Vow.

A CARNAL man does not understand why Paul so often boasts that he is an apostle of Jesus Christ according to the will of God. This boasting was as necessary to him in heavy temptation as an article of the faith. Satan had gained far more advantage over me, also, if I had not been a doctor by vocation.

It is not a little thing to change the whole religion and doctrine of the Papacy. How hard it was to me, will be seen in that Day; now no one believes it.

Gladly, at first, would I have subjected myself

to the Pope and his clergy; they, however, would not receive such humility and obedience from me, but insisted, as to-day, that I should give the lie to God, deny Christ, call His gospel heresy. Before I do that, I would, if God willed, and if it were possible, rather be burned ten times over.

In my baptism I promised my Lord Christ I would believe on Him, and cleave fast to Him. This, by His grace, working, and help, I will do. To this I keep in all my temptations (namely, to the vow which I made in baptism, which is the true and highest vow, that I would be faithful to Him), whereon He, on His part, promised He would be my God. If I had not had this consolation, I had long before fainted for great anguish in my heavy temptations. The dear Lord help further, Amen!

GOD speaks to me in His word through His ministers (as Christ says, "He who heareth you heareth Me"), and says to me, "I have baptized thee and received thee for my child, for Christ's sake, my beloved Son, who counted not His life dear unto Him to redeem thee. In him are hidden all the treasures of wisdom and knowledge, and these I give to thee to be thine own." This only comforts. If Christ is lost, all is lost in heaven and on earth.

IT is far too long a delay, if we wait to learn to know Christ until the last conflict. He came to us in baptism, and has been with us always, and has already made the bridge for us on which we pass from this life through death into the life beyond.

CHRIST was offered once for all; now He requires nothing but that we should give Him thanks forever.

HE who receives a sacrament does not perform a good work; he receives a benefit. In the mass we give Christ nothing; we only receive from Him.

IT is not the external eating which makes the Christian. It is the internal and spiritual eating which is the work of faith, and without which all external things are mere empty shows and vain grimaces.

This spiritual bread is the consolation of the afflicted, the cure of the sick, the life of the dying, food to the hungry, the treasure of the poor.

Preaching.

Preparation for Preaching.

DOCTOR MARTIN said to a pastor, "When you are about to preach, speak to God, and say, 'My Lord God, I wish to preach to Thine honor, to speak of Thee, to praise Thee, to glorify thy name.'"

Think not of me, nor of Philip, nor any of the learned, but remember you are then most learned in the pulpit when you speak of God. I have never been troubled because I could not preach well; but often, because I had to speak, before the face of God, of His great Majesty and Divine Being.

ONCE, when Dr. Martin sat under the pear-tree in his garden, he asked Magister Anthony Lauterbach how he prospered with his preaching? When he complained of his temptations, difficulties, and weakness, Dr. Martin said, "Ah, my friend, so it has been with me. I have dreaded the pulpit quite as much as you can; yet I had to go on.

"But you want to be a master all at once. Perhaps you are seeking honor, and are therefore tempted. You should preach for our Lord God, and not regard how men think and judge. If any one can do better, let him; do you preach Christ and the Catechism. Such wisdom will lift you above the judgments of all men, their praise or blame; for this wisdom is God's, wiser than men.

"You need not expect praise from me; if I hear you, I shall be sure to find fault; for you young (journeymen) preachers must be set down, lest you become ambitious and proud. But this thou shouldst ascertain; that thou art called to this, that Christ hath need of thee to help praise Him. On this stand firm; let who will praise or blame, that is not thy concern."

DR. MARTIN exhorted the clergy that they should not torture and detain their hearers with long sermons, "For," said he, "the pleasure of listening passes away from them; and the preachers do them hurt and violence with long preaching." "Some," said Dr. Martin, "plague the people with too long sermons; for the faculty of listening is a tender thing, and soon becomes weary and satiated."

HE was asked, "Which was the greater, to controvert adversaries, or to exhort and hold up the weak?"

He answered and said:

"Both are good and needful, although to comfort the faint-hearted is something greater; and yet the weak themselves are edified and improved by hearing the faith contended for. Each is God's gift."

YOU should not attempt to judge or criticise yourself. It often happens to me that I am ashamed of my sermon when I have finished it, and think how cold it has been; yet others have afterwards commended the same sermon much to me.

The Best Teachers always Learners.

IT is a true word in theology, that those who think they know anything know really nothing. For he who truly hears and learns

God's Word, can never wonder at it enough, or learn it to the bottom. Let every one humble himself and remain a learner therein.

Dr. Luther's Portrait of a good Preacher.

A GOOD preacher should have these virtues and qualities.

First, he should be able to teach plainly and in order.

Secondly, he should have a good head.

Thirdly, he should have good power of speech.

Fourthly, a good voice.

Fifthly, a good memory.

Sixthly, he should know when to stop.

Seventhly, he should be sure what he means to say, and should study diligently.

Eighthly, he should be ready to stake body and life, goods and glory, on its truth.

Ninthly, he must suffer himself to be vexed and criticised by everybody.

Keeping to the Point.

WHOEVER understands a subject thoroughly and intimately, can speak well about it.

"I endeavor in my sermons," said Dr. Martin, "to take a text and keep to it; and so to show it to the people, and spread it out before them, that they may say, 'This is what the sermon was about.' Soldiers should not greet every one they meet. Dr. Pommer is too much given sometimes to take with him everything he meets on his way. See what the main point is, and keep to it."

Simplicity.

LET all thy sermons be of the simplest. Look not to the princes, but to the simple, unwise, rude, and unlearned people; for the prince is made of the same stuff. If I in my sermons were to regard Philip Melanchthon and the other doctors, I should do no good; but I preach in the simplest way to the unlearned, and that pleases all. (I keep the Hebrew and Greek for the times when we learned men are alone together. Then we can talk such crabbed stuff they may well wonder at us in heaven.)

A PREACHER should have the skill to teach the unlearned, simply, roundly, and plainly; for teaching is of more importance than exhorting.

NO one should preach for me and Philip, however much we might learn from it. Preaching should not be magnificent with great, splendid, labored words, that men may see how learned we are. Ah, that is worth nothing. In the church every one should use the simple mother-tongue, such as every one can understand.

The doctors are present by forty, young people and unlearned by the thousand.

HE who has one word of God and cannot make a sermon out of it can never be a preacher.

TO preach simply is a high art. Christ does it himself. He speaks of husbandry, of sowing seed, and uses simple peasants' similes.

"ALBRECHT DURER, the famous painter," said Dr. Luther, "used to say he had no pleasure in pictures that were painted with many colors, but in those which were painted with a choice simplicity." So it is with me as to sermons.

IF I had to preach only to Dr. Hieronymus, or to Philip, I would not make another sermon my life-long, for they understand well enough already. Children, men-servants, and maid-servants attend our churches; to these we must preach; these need our preaching, not the learned. It is the poor young people and the simple with whom we have to do; to these we must come down.

So did the Lord Christ; He speaks as if for

His audience He had none other than my little Martin, Paul and Magdalene. When, indeed, He comes to the Pharisees, He gives them severe strokes.

We should preach to the little children; for the sake of such as these the office of preaching is instituted.

Dr. Martin said the best books of the Bible to preach from, were the Psalter, the Gospel of St. John, and St. Paul; but for the common people, and the young, the other Gospels.

WE must not teach the common people about high, difficult things, and with subtle words, for they cannot comprehend. Into the church come poor little children, maidens, old women and men, to whom such teaching is useless; and even if they say, " Ah, he said precious things; he made a fine discourse!" if one asks them further, " What did he say?" they often reply, " Ah, I do not know." To poor people we must call white, white, and black, black, all in the simplest way.

Ah, what pains our Lord Christ took to teach simply. From vineyards, sheep, and trees He drew His similes; anything in order that the multitudes might understand, embrace, and retain it.

Earnestness.

THIS is not the time for jest, but for earnest. " Ye are the salt of the earth." Salt bites and pains, but it cleanses and preserves from corruption.

Feeding and Guarding.

IN a true, good shepherd, feeding and guarding must be combined; for, if the guarding fails, the wolf will devour all the more readily the sheep which are well fed.

A preacher must be both a warrior and a shepherd. To feed is to teach, and that is the most difficult art; but it is needful also to be able to contend and defend.

The Best Kind of Controversy.

I COUNSEL those who preach in papal countries to teach the Gospel simply, without any snapping or biting. If they do this the Pope will fall, for he does not stand on the Gospel.

Religious Vanity, Gloria Religionis.

HE complained much of the vanity and self-sufficiency of the clergy, especially of the younger. "A new Jurist," he said, "is in his first year a Justinian; that is, he thinks himself superior to all the doctors, and has nothing but law in his head; the second year he is a Doctor; the third, a Licentiate; the fourth, a Bachelor; the fifth, a Student."

EVERY one should be content with his own gifts which God has given him; for we cannot all be Pauls and John Baptists; there must also be Tituses and Timothys. We need in any building more common stones than corner stones.

Excellence of the Office of the Preacher and Teacher.

HE who thinks lightly of preachers and of women will never come to good; as is commonly said. The office of the preacher, and women, the mothers of our children, must be held in all honor, that these be kept right and pure. The rule of the home and the State depends on them. Whosoever, therefore, despises these, and sets them at naught, despises God and man.

I WOULD wish that no one were suffered to be a preacher until he had first been a schoolmaster. Now, young men go at once from the school to the pulpit. But when any one has kept a school for ten years, he may leave it with a good conscience. The work is too heavy and too little esteemed. Yet a schoolmaster is as necessary in a town as a pastor. We might more easily do without burgomasters, princes, and nobles, than without schools, for these must govern the world.

No potentate or lord but needs to be guided by a jurist or theologian; and these come from schools.

If I were no preacher, I know no calling on earth that I should prefer to that of a schoolmaster. But we must not look at what the world rewards and esteems; we must consider what God esteems and will honor in that Day.

Trials and Burdens of the Preacher.

TO be a true pastor and preacher is a great thing; and if our Lord God Himself did not give strength, the thing could not be.

It needs a great soul to serve the people with body and soul, goods and honor, and to suffer for it the greatest peril and ingratitude.

Therefore it was that Christ said to Peter, "*Peter, lovest thou Me?*" and repeats it three times, and then says, "*Feed My sheep.*" It is as if He said: "If thou wilt be a true shepherd and friend of souls, thou must be so from love to Me." Otherwise it is impossible. For who will and can suffer ingratitude, spend his health and substance in study, and, for a reward, stand in the greatest peril? Therefore He says: "It is a necessity that thou shouldst love Me."

I HAVE begun, and I will persevere. I would not take the whole world to begin again, so exceeding great and heavy are the cares and sorrows of this office. Dear sirs, it is no child's play. Nevertheless, when I look at Him who has called me, I would not wish not to have undertaken it.

IF I were to write of the burdens which a preacher must bear, as I have experienced them, I should terrify every one from the office. A true God-fearing preacher must be so minded, that nothing is dearer to him than Christ his Lord and Saviour, and the future eternal life; so that when he has lost this life and all things, Christ may say to him, "Come hither to Me; thou hast been my good and faithful servant."

IT was once asked, when two preachers at Nürnberg had died of the Plague, "if a preacher, whose office is only preaching, may, with a good conscience, refuse his services to the sick, and not visit them in times of pestilence."

Thereupon Dr. Martin Luther answered and said:

"By all that is most sacred, No! The preachers must not flee too readily, lest they make the people fearful, and they should come to disregard the priests, seeing that at such a time none will come to them. It is not good, on the other hand, that all should stay.

"If the lot fell on me to stay, I would not shrink, nor fear. I have now survived three pestilences, and have been with many who have suffered; but, thank God, I took no harm. I came home and stroked my little Margarethe on the cheek, without washing my hands. But I had forgotten, or I would not have done it. It would have been tempting God."

ST. JEROME has written about the Book of Job; but he wrote only *thoughts*, for he had not experienced the deepest temptations (*i.e.*, spiritual, not fleshly). If I could have preached in my sickness, I could have made many a beautiful sermon on temptation; for then I learned to understand the Psalter and its consolations a little.

THE good Paul had to suffer and see many things, as God says of him: "*I will show him how great things he must suffer for My name's sake.*" He soon lays on his neck the *Pati*,—the yoke of suffering; and he experienced it indeed. Such heart-sorrow as is far worse than death. It is called *martyrum interpretativum*, martyrdom without blood, wherein we are indeed burned and tortured.

Rewards of the Preachers.

IF we are found true to our calling we shall receive honor enough; not, however, in this life, but in the life to come.

There we shall be crowned with the unfading crown of glory, as St. Paul says, which is laid up for us in heaven. But here on earth, saith the Lord Christ, we shall not have glory, for it is written: "*Woe unto you when all men speak well of you.*"

For we do not belong to this life, but are called to another, and a far better.

I will not be crowned on earth by men.

I choose to have my recompense from God, the just Judge, in heaven.

Patience as a Weapon.

Patience is the best Virtue.

IF thou wilt learn to overcome the greatest, fiercest, and most spiteful enemies, who would fain crush thee, and do thee all possible harm in body and soul, purchase before all things one weapon, and give all thou hast to learn how to exercise it. And know that it is one sweet, lovely little herb, which serves this purpose best, which is called *Patientia*.

"Ah," sayest thou, "how can I find this medicine?" The answer is, "Take faith to thee, which says that no one can hurt thee unless God wills it. If evil comes to thee, it comes to thee from God's kind and gracious will. So that thy foe does himself a thousandfold greater hurt than thee."

For from this faith flows love, which says: "I will still render good for evil, heap coals of fire on his head." This love is the Christian's armor and coat of mail, wherewith he casts down his foes, though they seem like great mountains, and are not to be cast down by iron and steel. This same love teaches us patiently to suffer all things.

NO one does me hurt, but it will hurt him in the end; for he has to die. I sin not in suffering, but he who makes me suffer, sins.

Patience with the Misled, and Anger against those who Mislead.

ST. PAUL showeth towards the Galatians a fatherly and motherly affection, and speaketh them very fair, and yet in such a sort that he reproveth them.

Contrariwise, he is very hot and full of indignation against those false apostles their seducers; he bursteth into plain thunderings and lightnings against them.

This example must we also follow, that we may show ourselves to bear like affection toward such as are misled.

But as for the devil and his ministers, against them we ought to be impatient, proud, sharp and bitter, detesting and condemning their false jugglings and deceits with as much rigor and severity as may be. So parents, when their child is hurt with the biting of a dog, are wont to pursue the dog only; but the weeping child they bemoan, and speak fair unto it, comforting it with the most sweet words.

IV.

THE ARMIES OF HEAVEN.

The Church.

"As it stands in the third article of our faith, one holy catholic—that is, universal—Church, the communion of saints."

THE Church is an assembly of people that depends on things which do not appear, nor can be apprehended by the senses; namely, on the Word alone. This people believes what the Word says, and gives God the glory of trusting that what He promises us therein is true.

THE Church is never in a more perilous state than when she has quiet and peace.

GOD has set His Church and Christian community in the midst of the world, amid infinite external action, manifold occupations, callings and standings, to the end that Christians should not be monks, nor fly into cloisters or wildernesses, but should live amongst people and be sociable, that their works of faith may be open and manifest.

To live in society and friendship with each other, as Aristotle the heathen says, is not indeed the end of man, whereunto he is created, but only a means to the end.

The most excellent end for which we are created is that one should teach another about God, what He is in His being, what His will is, how He is minded towards us.

Therefore let us in the Church, with the Church, pray for the Church. For there are three things which preserve the Church, and essentially belong to the Church: firstly, to teach faithfully; secondly, to pray diligently; thirdly, to suffer really (mit Ernst).

THE labor and travail of the Church lasts a long time; but one day her day and hour will come, that she shall be redeemed, and joyful indeed will be her aspect then.

THE outward form and aspect of the Church is without form or comeliness, sad and troubled; but in truth she is triumphing and gaining the victory with Christ. "He has set us in the heavenly places together with Christ." As a bride is Domina and lady of her husband's possessions, so is a believer lord of all the possessions of the Bridegroom ; for he is quickened with Christ, and set in heavenly places with Him.

God looks not on the evil in His Church, but only on Christ, His dear Son, whom He holds so dearly beloved, that for that love's sake He sees no evil in His Bride, for "He has cleansed her through the washing of water, by the Word."

Why the Church on Earth is in Tribulation.

FIRSTLY, that we should be reminded and warned that we are exiled servants, cast out of Paradise on account of Adam's fall in Paradise.

Secondly, that we may think of the sufferings of the Son of God, who for our sake became man, took our flesh and blood on Him, yet without sin, has walked through this valley of sorrows, has suffered and died for us, and has risen again from the dead, and has thus restored us to our Fatherland from which we were exiled.

Thirdly, that such tribulation might teach and remind us that our citizenship is not of this world, but that we here on earth are only pilgrims, and that another life, the life eternal, remains to us.

Amaranth a Type of the Church.

AMARANTH grows in August, and is more a stalk than a flower, is easily broken off, yet grows fair and flourishing after being broken. And when all the flowers are over, if this stalk is sprinkled with water and made moist it becomes fair again and green, so that in winter wreaths and garlands can be twined of it.

For this reason it is called amaranth, because it neither fades nor withers.

I know not that anything can be more like the Church than this amaranth, which we call a thousandfold fair (Tausendschön). For although the church washes her robes in the blood of the Lamb (as it is written in Genesis and in the Apocalypse), and is stained crimson, yet she is fairer than any state or community on earth. And she alone it is whom the Son of God loves as His Bride, in whom He has joy and rest.

Moreover, the Church suffers herself easily to be broken and crushed; that is, she is willing and contented to be obedient to God under the Cross, is patient therein, and springs up again fair and flourishing, and grows and spreads, yea, gains her best fruits and uses thence, for thereby she learns truly to apprehend God, freely to confess His doctrine, and brings forth far more beautiful and heavenly virtues.

Finally, the body and stock of this true Amaranth remain entire, and cannot be uprooted, however great may be the rage and assaults against particular branches, so as to rend them away. For as the amaranth, thousandfold fair, cannot fade nor decay, so nevermore can the

Church fade nor decay, be destroyed or rooted up. But what is more wonderful than the amaranth? If it is sprinkled with water and laid therein, it becomes green and fresh again, as if awakened from the dead.

So, we can have no doubt that the Church will be awakened by God from the grave, and will come forth living, eternally to praise, glorify, and bless the Father of our Lord Jesus Christ, and His son our Redeemer and Lord, with the Holy Ghost.

For although other empires, kingdoms, principalities, and dominions have their changes, and soon fade and fall away like flowers, this Kingdom, on the contrary, has roots so firm and deep, that by no force nor might can it be torn up or laid waste, but abides for ever.

None Suffer Alone.

WE are not alone. Many here and there in the world suffer with us, whom we know not.

THE saints are but as dewdrops on the locks of the Bridegroom.

HIS Christendom is Lady and Empress in heaven and on earth; for she is called the Bride of God.

The Holy Angels.

IT would not be fit that we should know how earnestly the dear, holy angels contend for us with the devil; what a hard and severe strife and warfare it is. For if we saw it, we should be dismayed.

"THEY are ministering spirits," and herein is set before all good Christians a great and heart-cheering truth, and a mirror of humility, that such pure and glorious creatures minister to us impure, poor, insignificant human beings, in the home, in the state, in religion.

Our faithful servants are they, rendering us service which we poor beggars and human creatures are ashamed to render another.

Thus should it be taught simply, and in choice order, concerning the dear angels.

THE good angels are wiser and can do more than the evil angels. The reason is, they have a mirror wherein they look and learn: "the face of the Father."

THEY are far nobler than we men; firstly, in nature and essence; also because they are without sin. But they are without pride; they despise not us human creatures for our misery. Our dying, sinning, and suffering are to them a sorrow of heart.

THE nature of the good angels is a humble, loving, and kindly nature. An angel's is a fine, tender, kind heart. As if we could find a man who had a heart sweet all through, and a gentle will; without subtlety, yet of sound reason; at once wise and simple. He who has seen such a heart, has colors wherewith he may picture to himself what an angel is.

THEY guard us from evil. This they do earnestly and with joy. The angels see nothing more gladly than when people delight in the Word of God. There they delight to dwell. Therefore seek them not yonder in heaven, but here below on earth, with thy neighbor, thy father and mother, thy child and thy friend. If thou dost to these as God commands thee, the angels will not be far from thee.

HE was once asked what an angel was. He said, "An angel is a spiritual creature, created without a body, by God, to minister to Christendom, especially in the offices of the Church. True and godly preachers should preach and teach concerning them in an orderly, Christian way."

THEIR antitypes are the evil spirits, which were not created evil by God, but fell, from a hatred which they conceived against God.

THE ARMIES OF HEAVEN.

DOCTOR MARTIN once said of the angels: "This is what I picture to myself, and I stand on it as on sure ground, that the angels are already getting ready for the field, drawing on their armor, girding on their sword and spear; for the Last Day is already beginning to dawn, and the angels are arming themselves for the combat.

IF we praise God that He has created for us the sun, the moon, wine, and bread, we should surely also praise Him that He has created the dear angels. My God, I thank Thee that Thou hast given Thy good angels, and hast set a guard of Thy heavenly princes round about us!

THE nature and character of the good angels is a humble, loving, friendly nature, which does not deem itself too high to serve poor sinful creatures, both men and women. For they are full of light, of the knowledge of God, and of the wisdom of the divine goodness. Therefore, all that God commands they understand to be perfect, and very good, because it pleases God.

LET us follow the virtues of the holy angels, and their works of love, and be very friendly, loving, and helpful to each other. No man is so kind, and so ready, and disposed to all kinds of services and good works as the angels are.

WE must learn that our best and most steadfast friends are invisible, namely, the dear angels, who with faithfulness and love, moreover with all helpfulness and true friendship, far surpass all the friends we have whom we can see. Thus in many ways we enjoy the fellowship of the heavenly spirits.

ANGELS are creatures who shine and burn with thoughts and desires how God can be praised, peace be on earth, and all men be of a good heart and mind.

His Belief about the Guardian Angel.

FROM early childhood I would accustom a child, and say to it: "Dear child, thou hast an angel of thine own. When thou prayest, morning and evening, the same angel will be with thee, and sit beside thy little bed, clothed in a white robe; will take care of thee, lull thee to sleep, and guard over thee that the evil one, the devil, may not come near thee. So, also, when thou gladly sayest the *'Benedicite'* and *'Gratias,'* at thy meals, thine angel will be with thee, at table, will serve thee, and guard thee." If we pictured this to children from their earliest years, that angels are with them, this would not only make the dear children trust to the guardianship of the dear angels, but it would make them gentle and good, for they would think, "If our parents are not here, the angels are here, and the evil one must not tempt us to do wrong."

AT the last, when we die, we have the dear angels for our escort on the way. They who can grasp the whole world in their hands, can surely also guard our souls, that they make that last journey safely.

V.

THE ENEMY.

The Devil.

THE serpent denies the good-will of God to us, and endeavors to persuade that God does not mean us well.

THE devil tempted Eve to all sin when he tempted her to resist the will of God.

The Devil the only Enemy to be hated.

"BLESS THOSE THAT CURSE YOU." How can ye do this? In no way better than by turning your eyes from the men who do you wrong, and fixing them on the wicked being who possesses them and urges them; on seeing how you can avenge yourselves, and cool your courage on him. He has not flesh and bones. He is a spirit. Therefore, as saith St. Paul, it is not against flesh and blood that ye have to fight, but against that spiritual villain above in the air, against the ruler of this dark, blind world.

WHEN it was once said to him, "I would fain know what the devil is like in character," Dr. Martin said, "If you see the true likeness of the devil, and know what his character is, give good heed to all the commandments of God, one after another, and represent to yourself a suspicious, shameful, lying, despairing, abandoned, godless, calumnious man, whose mind and thoughts are all set on opposing God in every possible way, and working woe and harm to others. Thus you may see the character of the devil."

FIRSTLY, in him is no fear, love, faith, and trust in God, that He is just, faithful, and true; but utter hatred, unbelief, despair, and blasphemy.

This is the devil's head set against the first commandment of the First Table.

Secondly, a faithful Christian uses the name of God to good uses, spreads His Word, calls on Him from the heart in need, praises Him, confesses Him.

But this wicked man does exactly the contrary; treats God's Word as a fable, blasphemes Him, curses men. There is the devil's mouth and speech.

Thirdly, a Christian holds the office of the

preacher dear, hears and learns God's Word with earnestness and diligence, receives the Holy Sacrament according to Christ's order. The other does the contrary, despises the preacher's office, hears God's Word not at all or carelessly. This is the devil's way of hearing.

Then for the Second Table.

A true Christian honors and obeys, for God's sake, parents, magistrates, those who have the care of souls, masters and teachers. The other obeys not parents, serves and helps them not, nay, dishonors, despises, and troubles them, forsakes them in their need, is ashamed of them when they are poor, despises them when they are old, infirm, and childish; obeys not authorities.

Again, a man of true heart envies not his neighbor, bears no ill-will against him, desires not revenge, has compassion when he is hurt, helps and protects him as much as he can. The other hates, envies, rejoices in his neighbor's troubles. There is the devil's grim, angry, and murderous heart.

A God-fearing man lives temperately and chastely; the other the contrary, in thought, word, and act.

A good man maintains himself by labor, trade, etc., lends, helps, and gives to the needy. The other takes every advantage. These are the devil's sharp claws.

Again, a good man speaks evil of no man—

yea, even if he knows that his neighbor is guilty, he covers his sin with love. The other back-bites, detracts, misinterprets, betrays. There is the devil's wicked will.

As our Lord God is *thesis decalogi*, so is the devil *antithesis decalogi*.

THE devil can indeed frighten, overwhelm, and kill; God alone can comfort and make alive. And that is His own prerogative and work. Therefore we do not know God at all unless we know Him as a Comforter of the wretched, troubled, and distressed, a Helper in need, who makes living and joyful. The true knowledge of God is to know that God is not a devil, *i. e.*, an accuser, an enemy, but only, entirely, and simply God, that is, only a Saviour.

WE have more cause to rejoice than to mourn; for our hope is in God, who says, "*I live, and ye shall live also.*" But melancholy is born with us; so the spirit of melancholy, the devil comes and stimulates it; but the Lord our God lifts us up.

WHEN one is on the battle-field with the devil, and is fighting against him, it is not enough to say, "That is God's Word." For this is one of the devil's master-strokes, to snatch the weapon from our hands, especially when he takes us by surprise. This he has often tried on me. He knows that my heart is always praying the Lord's Prayer, and yet he vexes me with the temptation that I have ceased to pray.

Let no one encounter him unless he prays the Lord's Prayer first. The devil is skilful, and we do not **know** the seven-hundredth part of what he knows. He **has assailed** Adam, Abraham, David, and others, and tormented **them in** manifold ways, and he knows where to attack us, where we are weak and he may give us a wound.

The Apostle Judas who betrayed Christ was throughout his life little assailed by the devil; but when the hour was come, he went securely forth on the devil's errand, and knew not whither.

HIS highest art is to make a law out of the Gospel; to represent the Lord Christ as a Judge and Accuser, and not as a Saviour, Mediator, High Priest, and Throne of Grace.

THE devil has a great advantage against us, inasmuch as he has a strong bastion and bulwark against us in our own flesh and blood.

THIS envious, poisonous, cunning spirit seeks to misinterpret and slander the good and godly works which a true Christian does through the grace of God, working and help of the Holy

Spirit. Therefore he is called *diabolus*, that is, accuser and slanderer.

AT night, when I wake, the devil is there, and wants to dispute with me. The evil one would dispute with me *de justitiâ;* and he is himself a villain, and would cast God out of heaven, and has crucified His Son.

THE devil has not indeed a doctor's degree, but he is highly educated and deeply experienced, and has moreover been practising, trying, and exercising his art and craft now wellnigh six thousand years. No one avails against him but Christ alone.

NO one can understand how to contend with him, unless he first pray with great earnestness. He is skilled in a thousand arts, and is far too strong and mighty for us, for he is the prince and god of this world.

THE devil seeks high things, looks to that which is great and high; scorns what is lowly. But the eternal merciful God reverses this, and looks on what is lowly. "I look on him who is poor and of a broken heart." But what is lifted up He lets go, for it is an abomination to Him.

THE devil, that lost spirit, cannot endure sacred songs of joy. Our passions and temptations, our complainings and our cryings, our Alas! and our Woe is me! please him well, but our songs and psalms vex him and grieve him sorely.

THE devil is a proud spirit. He cannot endure contempt. There is no better way to be quit of his temptations than by despising them (as Geroon says), just as when a traveller is attacked by a dog who would bite him; if the traveller goes quietly by, lets the dog howl and bark, and takes no heed of him, the dog does not bite him, and soon ceases to bark.

SATAN will not desist; he will contest every article of the faith in our hearts ere we depart this life, so bitterly opposed is he to the faith, which he well knows is the power and victory wherewith we overcome the world.

WE have the great devils who are doctors of theology (enemies of the First Table of the Decalogue). The Turks and Papists have little, insignificant devils to contend with, which are not theological but only juristical devils.

THE devil gives heaven before sin, and after we have sinned drives us to dismay of conscience, and to despair.

Christ does the contrary. He gives heaven after we have sinned, and peace to the troubled conscience.

ONE single devil is stronger and more cunning than all men, for they know us within and without, and compared with him we are only to be reckoned alphabet-scholars, poor and weak sinners, as we learn from experience.

FOR think only, if the devil in the beginning of the world was a bad creature, how cunning and skilful he must have become through such long practice, during which he has been assailing, and with all his power, without ever ceasing, has been tormenting Adam, Methuselah, Enoch, Noah, Abraham, David, Solomon, the prophets, the Apostles, yea, the Lord Christ Himself, and all believers.

THE devil has vowed our death. I hope, however, when he kills me, he will bite a deaf nut (*i. e.*, the kernel will be gone).

I SHOULD be so joyful that joy would bring me perfect health, and I could not be sick for mere joy. But the devil prowls incessantly about, makes me sad and careful, and when he cannot do it directly, does it through means; as for instance, through vexatious men.

THIS white devil, which urges men to commit spiritual sins, to sell them for righteousness, is far more dangerous than the black devil, which only tempts them to commit fleshly sins, which the world acknowledges to be sins.

SATAN'S power is greater than that of twelve Turkish Emperors; his knowledge greater than that of all men; his wickedness than that of the worst men; a powerful, able, subtle spirit.

THE kingdom of this world, or the devil's kingdom, is the kingdom of iniquity, ignorance, error, sin, death, blasphemy, desperation, and everlasting damnation. On the other side, the kingdom of Christ is the kingdom of equity, grace, light, remission of sins, peace, consolation, saving health, and everlasting life.

IT is strange that it should be commanded us, such weak flesh and blood as we are, to strive and fight with such a powerful spirit as the devil is, and that no other weapons should be placed in our hands, save only God's Word. This must irritate and vex such a great and mighty foe. But in such combats the hard thing is to recognize the devil as the devil.

God has ordered it thus, that when this mighty spirit is overcome simply by the faith of a good man, he may be all the more vexed and put to shame. That the "strong man armed" should be vanquished by one so weak, vexes him to the heart.

Warfare against all kinds of Evil—Warfare against the Devil

"I HOLD," he said, "that Satan sends epidemics and sicknesses amongst men, for he is a prince of death. Therefore St. Peter saith, 'Christ healed all who were held captive by the devil.'" To this end the devil uses natural means, poisonous air, &c., as a murderer uses a sword. So also God uses natural means to preserve man's health and life, as sleep and food.

A physician mends and repairs for our Lord God; he helps bodily, as we theologians spiritually, to make good what the devil has spoiled.

Once a burgomaster asked me if it was contrary to God to use medicine. (Doctor Carlstadt having publicly preached that in sickness we should use no medicine, but pray that God's will be done.) I asked him if he ate when he was hungry. "Yes," said he. Then I said to him, "Surely then you may use medicine, which is as much God's creature as food and drink, and all which we use to preserve this life."

Luther's own Experience in such Conflicts.

"LAST night," he said, "when I awoke, the devil came and wanted to dispute with me, and cast it up at me that I was a sinner. Then I said: Say something new, devil. That I know well already. I have committed real, actual sins. But God has forgiven me for His dear Son's sake."

THE devil often casts up against me that great offences have sprung from my doctrine. Sometimes he makes me heavy and sad with such thoughts. And when I answer that much good has also sprung thence, by a masterstroke, he can turn that against me. He is a swift, acute, cunning rhetorician.

How Luther met what he believed to be an Assault of the Devil.

ONCE, in the year 1521, when I had journeyed from Worms, and was imprisoned near Eisenach, in the castle of the Wartburg (in Patmos), I was far from any one, in a chamber to which no one was allowed to come save two young boys of the nobility, who twice a day brought me food and drink. Once they had brought me a bag of hazel-nuts, of which from time to time I ate, and had locked it up in a chest. At night when I went to bed, I put out the light. Then the hazel-nuts began to rattle against each other. But I did not heed. However, when I had been a little while asleep, such a clatter was made on the stairs, as if a score of platters had been thrown down from step to step, although I knew the staircase was guarded with chains and bolts, so that no one could come up. I rose and went to the head of the staircase and saw that all was closed. Then I said, "Oh, if it is only you, it does not matter." And I committed myself to the Lord Christ, of whom it is written, "Thou hast put all things under His feet," and lay quietly down in the bed again.

THANK God, the devil has never been able altogether to vanquish me. He has burnt himself out on the Lord Christ.

Sin.

SIN is essentially a departure from God.

THE first freedom is freedom from sin.

To Melanchthon, from Cobourg, during the Diet of Augsburg.

WHAT can the devil do worse than to kill us? I conjure thee, who art in all other things a good soldier, fight also against thyself, thy greatest enemy, who turnest Satan's arms against thyself.

WE have against us one-half of ourselves. The flesh striveth against the spirit.

THE recognition of sin is the beginning of salvation.

HELL is primarily forgetfulness, or hatred of God, for there reign a disordered, desolate, chaotic carefulness and self-love, unable to see the goodness and mercy of God; ever seeking escape and refuge from God.

ORIGINAL sin is the perversion of original righteousness.

WHERE sin is not acknowledged, there is no help nor remedy; for he who thinks himself whole when he is sick seeks no physician.

SIN is not forgiven that it may be no more felt, but that it may not be imputed.

UNKNOWN, hidden sins are the most dangerous. Therefore the prophet says, "Cleanse me from my secret faults."

THE sin against the Holy Ghost must be such a hidden, unacknowledged sin, not a coarse, worldly sin; but a deep spiritual sin. It must be a hardening in evil, or a contending against what is known to be truth, persevered in, without repentance until the end.

Especial Sins.

IT is a godless opinion and a vain dream to say that all sins are alike. St. Paul's sins were very different from Nero's.

Injustice.

TO THE ELECTOR FREDERICK, PLEADING FOR A POOR MAN HE DEEMED UNJUSTLY USED.

I KNOW well that no prince is so good but that he may deal too hastily with some, through his officials.

David was the kernel of all princes ever on the earth; yet he did wrong to poor Mephibosheth, at the demand of Ziba; thinking, however, that he had done him no wrong.

A prince may be sure his rule will be marred by injustice; well for him who does the least. Therefore are mercy and beneficence the more necessary.

Give, and it shall be given unto you. Where *Date* is rich, there *Dabitur* will be the richer.

Your Electoral Highness may be sure that I will not abandon this poor man thus. I will rather, myself, go begging for him. And if that did not answer, I would rob and steal whatever lay next me, especially from the Elector of Saxony. For your Electoral Grace is bound to maintain him.

To the Count Albert of Mansfeld

(Luther's native Prince), warning him against oppressing his subjects.

PEACE and grace in the Lord, and my poor Pater Noster.

Your Grace will graciously listen to my poor sighs, if, on account of the speaking and crying which I hear daily concerning my poor countrymen, I cannot begin my letter to your Grace cheerfully; for it is no fault of mine, and the child's heart in me is wounded. Your Grace must surely feel how cold you have become, and given over to Mammon, thinking only how to grow very rich; also (as the complaints go), bearing altogether too hard and sharply on your subjects, taking them from their fathers' inheritance, and their goods, and intending to make them mere bondmen.

Which God will not suffer, or if He suffer it, He will also suffer the whole country to be impoverished to utter ruin; for all things are His gifts, which He can easily withdraw again; and He is not bound to give account, as Haggai saith, "Ye have sown much, and bring in little; ye clothe you, but there is none warm; and he that earneth wages, earneth wages to put it into a bag with holes."

These things I write unto your Grace, as I think for the last time; for the grave is nearer me now, perhaps, than people think, and I entreat that your Grace will deal more softly and graciously with your subjects, and let them abide; so shall your Grace also abide, through God's blessing, here and yonder. Otherwise you will lose both together, and be like him of whom Æsop's fable speaks, who killed the goose which every day laid him a golden egg, and thereby lost at once the golden egg, with the goose, and all the egg stock;—be like the dog in Æsop, who lost the piece of flesh in the water while he was snapping at the shadow. For certainly it is true, that he who will have too much gains less; whereof Solomon in the Proverbs writes much.

In brief, I have to do with your Grace's soul, which I cannot bear to have cast out of my care and prayer; for this is to me sure: to be cast out of the Church is to be cast out of heaven. And hereto constrains me not only the command of Christian love, but also the heavy threat wherewith God has laden us preachers (Ezekiel 3d): "If thou warn not the sinner of his sin, and he die, I will require his soul at thine hands; for therefore have I set thee to be a watchman of souls."

Therefore, may your Grace take this needful warning in good part; for I cannot on your Grace's account suffer myself to be damned; but seek much rather to save you with myself, if it is by any means possible. But before God, I am hereby free from guilt concerning this.

Herewith I commend you to Him in all His grace and mercy. Amen.

Falsehood.

A LIE is like a snow-ball. The longer it is rolled, the larger it is.

Covetousness.

MAMMON has two virtues; the first, that he makes us secure when things go well, so that we live without the fear of God.

The second, that in adversity, when things go ill, he teaches us to tempt and fly from God, and to seek a false god.

IT was with good reason that God commanded through Moses that the vineyard and harvest were not to be gleaned to the last grape or grain; but something to be left for the poor. For covetousness is never to be satisfied; the more it has, the more it wants. Such insatiable ones injure themselves, and transform God's blessings into evil.

RICHES are the pettiest and least worthy gifts which God can give a man. What are they to God's Word? Yea, to bodily gifts, such as beauty and health; or to the gifts of the mind, such as understanding, skill, wisdom? Yet men toil for them day and night, and take no rest. Therefore our Lord God commonly gives riches to foolish people to whom He gives nothing else.

JEROBOAM'S calves remain in the world forever until the Last Day; for whatever a man places his confidence and trust in, setting God aside, that is to him like Jeroboam's calves, which he worships and invokes instead of the only true, living, eternal God, who alone can and will give counsel and help in all need.

All are worshipping these calves who trust to their own skill, wisdom, strength, holiness, riches, honor, power, or to any league, defence, or fortress, or in brief to anything, be it called what it may, on which the world builds and trusts. For such trust in transitory creatures is the real idolatry.

LIES drowned and overwhelmed in the sea of covetousness, deeper than the mountains under the flood; these lay only fifteen ells deep in the water, but she lies fifteen miles deep under the waves of avarice.

THE Jews suffered themselves to dream, and thought that the kingdom of Christ would be a worldly kingdom; as also the Apostles in John 14: "*Lord, how is it that thou wilt manifest Thyself unto us, and not unto the world?*"

"We thought the whole world should see Thy glory; that Thou shouldst be Cæsar, and we twelve kings, amongst whom the kingdoms should be divided; that each of us should have had six disciples for princes, counts, and nobles; these would be the seventy-two disciples—for that was the number." Thus had the dear Apostles already beautifully parcelled out the land, according to Platonic dreams and human reason.

But Christ describes His kingdom far otherwise: "*He who loveth Me, and keepeth my Word, shall be loved of my Father; and we will come unto him, and make our abode with him.*"

IT is a terrible evil, that we see daily before our eyes, how eager a thirsty man is to drink, and a hungry man to eat, although a drink of water and a piece of bread can only keep off thirst or hunger an hour or two; whilst on the contrary no one, or scarcely any one, is eager for this most precious Physician, although He tenderly allures all to Him, saying, "*If any man thirst, let him come unto Me and drink,*" and gives food and drink which are imperishable, and endure to eternal life.

WE know, thank God, that Christ has overcome the world, with her prince the devil; that sin may no more have dominion over us, nor death swallow us up. At which we should, in reason, be far more joyful than the children of the world over temporal prosperity, riches, honor, power. For these, be they as much as they may be compared with the eternal riches which Christ gives, are indeed mere trifling, contemptible fragments and crumbs.

IF we have Him, the dear Lord, we are indeed rich and happy enough, and ask not for their pomp, glory, and wealth. Too often, indeed, we lose Him, and consider not that He is ours, and we are His ; especially when, in time of need, He seems to hide His face for a moment. But He says, "*I am with you alway to the end of the world.*" This is our best treasure.

WHERE the Gospel is, there is poverty. In olden times men could richly endow whole convents; now they will give nothing. Superstition, false doctrine, and hypocrisy give money enough. Truth goes begging.

Carefulness.

"THEY SOW NOT, NEITHER DO THEY REAP, NOR GATHER INTO BARNS."

Let the Lord build the house, and be the householder. He who filleth heaven and earth can surely fill one house.

If thou dost not look to Him who should fill the house, every corner of it must indeed be empty to thee. But if thou art looking to Him, thou perceivest not if there be an empty corner. To thee all seems full, and indeed all is full. If not, it is the defect of thy vision, as with the blind, who see not the sun.

Not that labor is forbidden, but that God gives success. For if thou wert to plough a hundred years, thou couldst not bring one stalk out of the earth. But God, without work of thine, whilst thou art asleep, creates out of the little grain a stalk, and on the stalk many ears, as many as He wills.

The animals do not work in order to earn their food; yet each has its work. The bird flies and sings, and hatches its eggs; that is its work. Horses carry men on the road, and to the battle; sheep give us wool, milk, and cheese; that is their work; yet that feeds them not. The earth freely brings forth grass and feeds them, through God's blessing. Thus Christ tells us to behold the fowls of the air; they sow not, neither do they reap, nor gather into barns, and yet God feedeth them. That is, they do their appointed work, but not thereby are they fed.

So also must man work. But let him know, it is Another that feeds him, namely, God blessing his work.

This is the signification of it all. God commanded Adam to eat bread in the sweat of his brow, and wills that men shall work, and without work will give them nothing. On the other hand, by our work, in itself, He gives us nothing, but only of His free goodness and blessing; that labor may be our discipline in this life, to overcome the flesh.

You say, Who places the silver and gold in the mountains, that men may find them? Who places in the field those great hidden treasures which spring out of it in corn, wine, and all manner of fruits, whereby all creatures live? Does man's labor create these? Man's labor indeed finds them; but God has laid the treasures there, and He bestows them.

Thus the ruler must indeed watch over the city, close the gates, guard tower and wall, put on armor, lay up stores, as if there were no God. And the householder must work as if his work in itself were to nourish the household. But he who believes in God is not careful for the morrow, but labors joyfully and with a great heart.

"For He giveth His beloved, as in sleep." They must work and watch, yet never be careful or anxious, but commit all to Him, and live in serene tranquillity; with a quiet heart, as one who sleeps safely and quietly.

(The last letter to her but one.)

To the holy, care-laden lady, Katharin Lutherin, my gracious, dear Wife.

WE thank you very heartily for the great care for us, which has prevented your sleeping; for since the time that you have taken this care on you, the fire all but consumed us in our inn, breaking out outside our chamber door, and yesterday (no doubt in consequence of these cares of yours), a stone all but fell on our head and crushed us, as in a mouse-trap; for in our room, two days since, the lime and plaster crumbled away. * * For this also we should have had to thank your saintly cares, if the dear holy angels had not hindered. I am anxious lest, if thou dost not give up thy anxieties, the earth itself may swallow us up, and all the elements turn against us.

Dost thou learn the Catechism, and the Creed? Do thou pray, and leave God to care. It is said, "*Cast your care on Him, for He careth for you.*"

Temptation, and Depression of Spirit.

For one heavy in Heart.

FIRST of all, let her not look at herself, nor judge herself by her own feelings, but grasp the Word, and hang upon it, and plant herself on it, in defiance of all, and direct all her feelings, and all the thoughts of her heart towards it.

Let her also lift up her voice in praise. A strong medicine lies therein.

For the evil spirit of heaviness is not to be chased away by sad words and complainings, but by the praise of God, whereby the heart is made glad.

YOUR distress is, that God Almighty knows from eternity who will be saved. Which is true; for he knows all things, the drops in the sea, the stars in heaven, the roots, branches, twigs, and leaves of every tree. He has numbered the hairs of our heads. From this you conclude that do what you will, good or bad, God knows already whether you will be saved or not. And further, you think more of damnation than of salvation, and therfore you despair, and know not how God is minded toward you.

Wherefore I, as a servant of my dear Lord Jesus Christ, write you this, that you may know how God the Almighty is minded toward you.

God, the Almighty, does know all things; so that all works and thoughts in all creatures must happen according to His will. But His earnest will, and mind, and decree, ordered from eternity, is "*that all men shall be saved,*" and shall become partakers of eternal joy. "*God willeth not the death of a sinner, but that he should be converted and live.*"

If, therefore, He wills that sinners, wherever they live and wander under the broad, high heavens, should be saved, will you, by a foolish thought suggested by the devil, sunder yourself from all these, and from the grace of God?

God the Father Himself, with His own finger,

points out to you how He is minded toward you, when with loud clear voice He cries, "*This is my beloved Son in Whom I am well pleased. Hear Him.*"

And even if you were ever so hard and deaf, and as a despairing man turned to stone, could not look up to heaven, nor hear God the Father calling to you on those heights, yet can you not fail to hear the Son, who stands in the highway by which every one must pass, and as with a mighty trumpet calls, "*Venite!*" "Come, come!"

But who are those who are to come? "*Ye that are weary and heavy-laden.*" What kind of a company is that? "Heavy-laden;" as if He knew it all well, and would take our burdens and loads on His shoulder, and not only help us, but altogether rid us of them.

To Hieronymus Weller.

IN AN ATTACK OF DEPRESSION.

THEREFORE, before all things, thou shalt firmly hold, that those and evil thoughts are not from God, but from the devil; because God is not the God of sadness, but the God of consolation and gladness, as Christ Himself says, "*He is not the God of the dead but of the living.*" But what is to live save to be glad in the Lord?

WHEREFORE use thyself at once to repel such thoughts, saying, "*The Lord hath not sent thee."* Hard is the fight at the beginning; but use makes it easier. It is not thou alone who endureth such thoughts, but all the saints; yet they have fought and conquered. So also thou, yield not to evil, but go forth bravely. The highest valor in this fight is not to look at these thoughts nor to investigate them, but to disperse them like a flock of geese, and to pass by. He who has learnt this has conquered; he who has not learnt it will be conquered. For to gaze at them, and dispute with them until they cease, or freely yield, is but to irritate and to strengthen them.

Let Israel be an example to thee, who overcame the fiery serpents, not by gazing or by struggling, but by averting their gaze, and looking at the brazen serpent. This is the true and certain victory in this combat. Therefore take heed, my Jerome, that thou suffer them not to linger in thy heart. Thus a certain wise man replied to one so tempted, who said "Such and such sad thoughts have come into my mind," by saying, "Then let them go again." And another, as a wise oracle said, "Thou canst not prevent the birds from flying above thy head; but thou canst prevent their building their nests in thy hair."

To Barbara Lischnerinn.—1530.

VIRTUOUS dear Lady:—Your dear brother, Hieronymus, Weller has told me how you are troubled with temptations about the eternal foreseeing of God. That is truly grievous to me. Christ, our Lord, will redeem you from this. Amen.

For I know this sickness well, and have lain sick to eternal death in that hospital.

First, you must grasp firmly in your own heart that such thoughts come from the devil and are his fiery darts.

Secondly, when such thoughts come, you should ask yourself " In what commandment is it written that I should think of these things ; Thou, O devil, wouldst have me care for myself, but I must cast my care on God, for He careth for me."

Among all the commands of God, this is the highest that we should picture to ourselves His dear Son, our Lord Jesus Christ, Who is to our hearts the daily and most excellent mirror wherein we see how dear God holds us.

Here we learn God's Providence, by believing in Christ. If you believe, you are called ; if you are called, you are also predestinated. Let none tear Christ, this mirror and throne of grace, from your heart.

TO the heavy temptations concerning eternal election which so deeply distress many, nowhere is such a solution to be found as in the Wounds of Christ. " *This is My beloved Son ; hear Him.* In Him you will find Who and what

I am, and what I will; and nowhere else in heaven or on earth."

The Father has fixed a sure and firm foundation on which we can firmly rest—Jesus Christ our Lord, through Whom we must enter the Kingdom of Heaven. For He, and none else, is the Way, the Truth, and the Life.

To Valentine Hausmann.—1532.

I HAVE heard of your heaviness through inward terrors; but you must not distress yourself much on this account; for God is wonderful in His way toward us, so that things seem to us often bad and hurtful which are really most useful to us, although we understand not how. Who knows what worse might have come to you, if God had not thus taken you under His discipline, and kept you in His fear? Therefore you must not be impatient although your faith be not strong. For St. Paul says the weak in faith are not to be rejected. God is not a Father who casts out sick and diseased children. If He were, He would keep none. Therefore you should say to Him, "Dear Father, if it pleases Thee thus to chastise me, I will be content to have it so. Thy will be done; only give me patience."

For the rest, I know not how you are meeting this; for you should be calling on God and praying; especially when you feel the terror is coming, fall on your knees and cry to heaven; and although the prayer seem to you in vain, and too cold, do not for that give over. Strike a firm stroke, and pray so much the more earnestly, the more it seems to you in vain.

For you must learn to fight and not to keep still and gaze, or suffer whatever this temptation inflicts, until it ceases of itself. For that way will only gain strength. You must pray mightily, and call aloud, and with ringing words cry out the Our Father.

And before all things you have to grasp in your heart the conviction that this is from the devil, whom God will have us resist.

But if, indeed, you cannot pray, let something be read to you from the Psalms or the New Testament, with a clear voice; and listen to it. For you must use yourself, at such times, not to wrestle with the anguish in your own thoughts, without God's Word; you should hear the voice of prayer and God's Word together.

For without God's Word the foe is too strong for us. But prayer and the Word of God he cannot endure.

To Jonas von Stockhausen.—1532.

IT has been shown me by good friends how the malignant enemy is assailing you sorely with weariness of life, and longing for death.

You know we must be obedient to God, and diligently guard ourselves against disobedience to His will. Now you are sure God has given you life, and has not yet willed you to be dead. Therefore you can have no doubt that such disobedient thoughts come from the devil; and that with all your might you must tear them out.

Life was sour and bitter to our Lord Christ; yet He would not die except by the Father's will, and fled from death and held to life whilst He could, and said, "*My hour is not yet come.*"

Elias, indeed, and Jonas, and other prophets, called and cried for death, from great anguish and impatience of life; cursed even the day of their birth. Yet they had to live and bear this weariness with all their strength, until their hour was come.

Such words and examples as the Holy Ghost's words and warnings you must faithfully follow, and the thoughts which drive you thence you must cast out and spit upon. And although this may be sour and bitter to do, you should but think of yourself as one bound and held captive with chains, out of which you must twist and writhe yourself, with sweat of anguish. For the devil's darts, when they pierce so deep, are not to be torn out with laughter, or without labor. They must be wrenched out by main force. You must gnash your teeth against these thoughts, and set your face as a flint to do God's will, harder than iron or anvil.

Yet the best counsel of all is that you should scorn these temptations, and make as if you did not feel them, and think of something else, and say to the devil, "Come, then, devil! let me alone! I cannot listen to thy thoughts. I have to travel, eat, drink, ride, or do this or that."

Herewith I commend you to our dear Lord, the only Saviour and true Conqueror, Jesus Christ.

To the Lady von Stockhausen.

THE devil is an enemy to both you and your husband, because you hold Christ, his enemy, dear.

See that you do not leave your husband a moment alone. Solitude is pure poison for him. It would do no harm to read to him histories, news, and all kinds of strange things, even if they were gloomy or false tidings and tales, about the Turks, Tartars, and the like, if he could be made to laugh and jest about it. And thereon soon follow with comforting words of the Scriptures.

Whatever you do, do not let him be alone or dull, so that he sink into thought. Never mind if he is angry at this. Pretend that you are suffering, and complain about it.

Christ, who is the cause of the devil's enmity and your heart-trouble, will help you. Only hold fast to this, that you are the apple of His eye. Who touches you touches Him.

To Johann Schlaginhausen.—1533.

I HEAR with pain that you are sometimes troubled in mind, although, indeed, Christ is as near to you as yourself, and will surely do you no harm, since He has shed His blood for you. Dear friend, give honor to this good, faithful Man, and believe that He holds you dearer, and has more favor to you than Doctor Luther, and all Christians.

What you trust us to be, trust Him to be far more.

For what we do, we do at His bidding. But He who bids us do it, Himself does all unbidden, from His own spontaneous goodness and kindness.

To Joachim, Prince of Anhalt.—1534.

WE know not what we should pray for as we ought, but He, as a faithful Father, knows and sees well how we should pray, and does according to what He knows, not according to how we pray.

Thus indeed a father must deal with his child, not giving what the child asks, but what he knows the child should ask. Although the child weeps for it, that does not hurt him; nor is the child's request less dear to the father because he does not give in the way the child desires.

So also, often, the physician must not do what the patient wishes, and yet he holds the sick man none the less dear for his sick longings and for the request he cannot grant.

* * * *

I counsel you also (as a remedy against this depression) to ride, hunt, and occupy yourself as a young man should, in good company, who can be merry with you in a godly and honorable way.

To Johann Mantel,

SERVANT OF THE CHURCH AT WITTENBERG.

AS to what you write about temptation and sadness on account of death, you know how in our faith we express and confess that the Son of God suffered under Pontius Pilate, was crucified and died to this end, that He might, for all who believe in Him, take away the power from death, yea altogether and utterly abolish it. Dear friend, what great matter is it that we shall die, when we really think that He, the dear Lord has died, and has died for us? His death is the true, only death which should so possess and fill our hearts, senses and thoughts, that it should henceforth be to us no otherwise than as if now nothing was living any more, not even the dear sun, but that all died with the dear Lord; yet died in such a way that all with Him shall rise again at that blessed day.

In this His death and life, our death and life should sink and be swallowed up, as those who shall live with Him forever.

And truly from the beginning of the world He has been before us with His death; and to even the end of the world. He waits for us when we shall depart out of this brief, poor life, and He shall welcome us and receive us into His eternal kingdom.

To a Pastor.

ALAS, we live in the kingdom of the devil, *ab extra*, therefore we cannot hear or see any good, *ab extra*. But we live in the blessed Kingdom of Christ *ab intra*. There we see, though as in a glass darkly, the exceeding unutterable riches of the grace and glory of God.

Therefore, in the name of the Lord, let us break through, press forward, and fight our way through praise and blame, through evil report and good report, through hatred and love, until we come into the blessed kingdom of our dear Father, which Christ the Lord has prepared for us before the beginning of the world. There only shall we find joy. Amen.

GOD forbid that the offence of the Cross should be taken away; which thing would come to pass if we would preach that which the prince of this world and his members would gladly hear. Then we should have a gentle devil, a gracious pope, and merciful princes. But because we set forth the benefits and the glory of Christ, they persecute us and spoil us both of our goods and lives.

I DID not learn my theology all at once; but I have had to search ever deeper and deeper into it. To this many conflicts have brought me, for no one can understand the Holy Scriptures without exercise and conflict. Fanatics and pretenders, each the true adversary, namely the devil, who with his buffetings drove me to study the Holy Scriptures. If we have no such devil, we are only speculative theologians, who rove about in their own thoughts, speculating that thus and thus it must be.

Yet no good art or handicraft is to be learned without exercise. What kind of a physician would he be who perpetually did nothing but roam about the schools? He must bring his art into practice, and the more he has to do with nature, the more he sees and experiences how imperfect his art is.

It is a great grace of God to be able to say of one text in the Bible, "That I know for certain to be true."

I know, old and learned Doctor that I am (or ought to be), that I have not yet mastered the Lord's Prayer. Without exercise and experience no one can become truly learned.

THIS will not be thy greatest nor thy last temptation. The wisdom of God is, as it were, playing with thee and training thee, if thou livest, for real war.

IT is a hard thing to say always, I am God's child; and to be comforted and refreshed by the great grace and mercy of the heavenly Father. To do this from the heart is not what every one can do. Therefore, without exercise and experience, no one can learn the faith in true purity.

THE Holy Spirit cheers us, and teaches us to despise death and all dangers. He says (in us), "If God wills not that I should live, then I will die; if He wills not that I should be rich, I will be poor." But the evil spirit saddens and terrifies, at the last, after making secure and self-satisfied. Joyfulness comes from God, depression from the devil.

CONFLICT makes us live in the fear of God, walk circumspectly, pray without ceasing, grow in grace and in the knowledge of Christ, and learn to understand the power of the Word.

Therefore be not faint-hearted, nor dismayed; but take such conflicts for a sure sign that thou hast a gracious God, since thou art being fashioned into the likeness of His Son; and doubt not that thou belongest to the great and glorious brotherhood of all the Saints, of whom St. Peter says, "Resist the devil, steadfast in the faith, knowing that the same afflictions are accomplished in your brethren which are in the world."

THE essence of temptation is that we forget the present, and covet the future, like Eve in Paradise.

ALL do not suffer the same temptations. Indeed they could not. Some must be knuckles and bones which can sustain and keep together the flesh. Just as in the body of man, if all were flesh it would fall into a shapeless mass. The knuckles and nerves hold the flesh together. So, in the Christian Church, there must be some who can sustain good buffetings from the devil; such as we three, Philip Melanchthon, Doctor Pommer, and I. But all could not bear it. Therefore, in the Church we pray one for another. Prayer does all things.

DOCTOR MARTIN said to Schlainhaeffen, "Fear not, neither be dismayed. All will turn to the best for you; your trial will work for God's glory, and for the profit and health of us all.

"It is impossible that man's heart can know God truly and keep Him in mind without the cross and temptation. Believe me, if you had not such a good stone in God the Father's house, you would not have these conflicts."

ONLY believe firmly God will make an end of this trial. For He calls that which is not, that it may be. As I have myself experienced in sore temptations, which so exhausted and tortured my body that I could scarcely breathe, went about like a shadow, like a corpse, withered, parched up, and no man could comfort me. All to whom I spoke, said "I know not." No confessor could understand anything of it, so that I said, "Am I, then, alone? Is it I only who must be thus sorrowful in spirit and thus assailed?"

Dr. Staupitz said to me at table, seeing me so sad and smitten down, "Why are you so sad, brother Martin?" Then I said, "Whither shall I flee?" He answered, "Ah! know you not that such temptation is good for you? Otherwise no good could come of you."

Ten years ago, when I was alone, God comforted me through His dear angels, with my own striving and writing.

Therefore fear not; you are not alone.

BISHOP ALBERT of Mainz used to say that "the human heart is like a mill-stone in a mill. If you place corn on it, it spins round, grinds, and crushes, and makes it into meal. If there is no corn it still spins round, and grinds itself, so that it becomes thinner and smaller. So the human heart must have work to do; if it has not the work of its calling to fulfil, the devil comes with temptation, heaviness, and sadness, till the heart devours itself with sorrow."

In his own Sickness.

"AH, how gladly would I now die. For I am now weary and worn out, and have a peaceful and joyful conscience and heart. But I know, as soon as I recover, care, toil, and temptation will not keep outside. For through much tribulation we must enter into the Kingdom of God."

IN the year 1538, on the night of the 2d of August, Doctor Martin Luther had a severe pain in his arm, as if it were being torn. Then he said, "Thank God! That we can say, for it is an easier thing to yield up our money, or our skin. But when spiritual temptations come, that we could say, 'Cursed be the day wherein I was born!' that does give pain! In such trial was Christ, in the Garden: '*Father take this cup from Me!*' There was the will against the will."

DOCTOR MARTIN once said to a very desponding man, "Oh, friend, what art thou doing? Canst thou do nothing but look at thy sins, thy death, and damnation? Turn thine eyes quite the opposite way, and look at Him who is called Christ. Of Him it is written that He was conceived of the Holy Spirit, born of the Virgin Mary, suffered, died, and was buried, descended into hell, on the third day rose again from the dead, ascended into heaven. Why, dost thou think, did all this happen? That thou mightest be comforted against death, and sin. Therefore cease to fear and to be dismayed. Verily thou hast no cause. If Christ were not there, and had not done all this for thee, then indeed thou mightest fear."

SEE what a life the Lord Christ led whilst He went about on earth. He was not much alone; there was ever a noise and stir of much people around Him. He was never alone, save when He was praying. So He has promised, "Where two or three are gathered together in My name, there am I in the midst of them."

KING DAVID, when he was alone and idle, and went not forth to the war, fell into temptation. God created man for society, and not for solitude.

DR. LUTHER said that often when he was tempted, a word from a good friend had comforted him: "For when, in the year 1535, I was much troubled about something, and cast down, Doctor Pommer said to me, 'Our Lord God doubtless thinks in heaven, "What shall I do more with this man? I have given him so many great and noble gifts, and still he will despair of my goodness."'

"These words were a glorious, great comfort

to me, and took fast hold of my heart, as if an angel from heaven had spoken them to me, although Dr. Pommer thought not to comfort me with them."

IN the year 1541 Doctor Luther was recalling his spiritual temptation in his sickness, when for fourteen days he neither ate, drank, nor slept. "At that time I disputed with our Lord God in wild impatience, and reproached Him with His promises. Then God taught me to understand the Holy Scriptures aright; for when all goes according to our will we do not know much of God's Word. Now God will not have us be too impatient; therefore in His Holy Scriptures He requires us frequently to hope and wait on Him, as in the Psalm, 'I wait on the Lord from one morning watch to another.' For if God does not help speedily, yet He gives grace to sustain temptation. So Job says, '*Though He slay me I will trust in Him*,' just as if he said, 'Though it seems as if Thou hadst turned away Thy face from me, yet I will never believe Thou art my enemy.'"

A NUN, who was sorely tempted, and had no other weapons wherewith to drive away the devil, said, "I am a Christian; that word contains everything in itself."

GOD has set a firm ground for us to tread on, and thereby to ascend into heaven, even Jesus Christ. He only is the way and door by which we come to the Father. But we want to begin our building with the roof; we despise the foundation, and therefore we must fall.

AH, if that great man, Paul, were living now, how glad I should be to learn from him what his thorn in the flesh was. It was not a beloved Thekla, as the legends say. Oh no! It was not a sin. I know not what it was.

The Book of Job is full of such temptations. His friends and comforters were sensible, prudent, wise, just, and pious people; yet they did not touch the point. For around this turns the whole debate in the book. "I am just and innocent," says Job. They say, on the contrary, "Ah! that is of the devil, to say that thou art good and just. Then God must be unjust!" Round this question revolves the whole controversy. I hold that the Book of Job is a history, afterward worked into a poem, concerning things which were actually experienced by some one; although not uttered in the words in which it is described.

It is a good book, and therein we have a choice picture and example of an assaulted and troubled Christian. For this book was not written with reference to Job, or any individual, but is a mirror for all suffering Christians. We see in it what kind of a process God is carrying on through the trials of the Saints. For when it is only the devil and the Chaldeans, Job can be patient, and says, "Blessed be the name of the Lord." But when it is a question of God's anger, he can no longer bear it, and falls into perplexity and disputing about the happiness of the ungodly.

But he worked his way out of this perplexity again and said, "I know that Thou art good." Although it is hard to say it. In brief, all men have flesh and blood in them which murmurs and sets itself against God; for it is hard to believe, when we are in trial, that God is gracious to us.

Part Second.

WORDS FOR THE DAY'S MARCH.

WORDS FOR THE DAY'S MARCH.

I.

THE LEADER.

FOR the rest, I am expecting daily the maledictions of Rome. I am disposing and arranging all things, so that when these arrive I may go forth prepared and girded; like Abraham not knowing whither, or rather knowing most certainly whither, since God is everywhere.—1518.

WHAT a beautiful, comforting Gospel that is in which the Lord Christ depicts Himself as the Good Shepherd; showing what a heart He has toward us poor sinners, and how we can do nothing to save ourselves.

The sheep cannot defend nor provide for itself, nor keep itself from going astray if the shepherd did not continually guide it ; and when it has gone astray and is lost, it cannot find its way back again nor come to its shepherd ; but the shepherd himself must go after it, and seek it until he find it ; otherwise it would wander and be lost forever. And when he has found it he must lay it on his shoulder and carry it, lest it should again be frightened away from himself, and stray, or be devoured by the wolf.

So also is it with us. We can neither help nor counsel ourselves, nor come to rest and peace of conscience, nor escape the devil, death, and hell, if Christ Himself, by His word, did not fetch us, and call us to Himself. And even when we have come to Him, and are in the faith, we cannot keep ourselves in it, unless He lifts and carries us by His Word and power, since the devil is everywhere and at all times on the watch to do us harm. But Christ is a thousand times more willing and earnest to do all for His sheep than the best shepherd.

Not at our own Will.

I CANNOT guide myself, and yet would fain guide the world ! Many a time I have made fine articles and rules, and brought them to our Lord God to guide Him. But the good God has let me see in the end how all my mastering has come to nothing.

Not at our own Pace.

THIS temptation oftentimes excuseth the godly, that their life seemeth unto them to be rather a certain slow creeping than a running. But if they abide in sound doctrine and walk in the spirit, let this nothing trouble them. God judgeth far otherwise.

For that which seemeth unto us to be very slow, and scarcely to be creeping, is running swiftly in God's sight. Again, that which is to us nothing else but sorrow, mourning, and death, is before God joy, goodness, and true felicity.

The Word of God as Daily Bread.

ALTHOUGH the works of God are not dumb, but picture Him to our eyes that we may see Him, yet He comforts us far more powerfully when He adds to His works a living Word, which the eyes do not see, but the ears hear, and the heart, through the inworking of the Holy Spirit, understands.

"The Divine Art of Learning."

I ALTHOUGH I am an old Doctor of the Holy Scriptures, have not yet come out of the children's lessons; and do not yet rightly understand the Ten Commandments, the Creed, and the Lord's Prayer. I cannot study or learn them through and through, but I am learning daily therein; and I pray the Catechism with my son Hans, and with my little daughter Magdalene.

When, indeed, do we understand in its breadth and depth the first words of the Lord's Prayer, "*Who art in heaven*"? For if I understood and believed these few words, that God, who has created heaven and earth, and all creatures, and has them in His hand and power, is my Father, then would follow this sure conclusion, that I should also be a lord of heaven and earth; that Christ should be my brother, and all things be mine. Gabriel must be my servant, and Raphael my guide, and all angels must minister to me in my needs.

But now, that my faith may be exercised and preserved, my Father in heaven lets me be thrown into a dungeon, or fall into the water. In such trials we see and experience how far we understand these words, how our faith totters, and how great our weakness is.

Therefore, the one little word, "*Thine*" or "*Our*," is the hardest word in the Holy Scriptures, as is to be seen in the first Commandment, "*I am the Lord thy God.*"

TO fathom and truly to exhaust one single word in the Holy Scriptures is impossible. I defy all learned men and theologians to do it.

For they are the words of the Holy Spirit; therefore they are too high for all men; and we new-born Christians have only the first-fruits, not the tithe.

I have many times thought of commenting on the Ten Commandments, but when I have only begun with the first word, which sounds thus, "*I am the Lord thy God,*" I have stopped short at the little word "*I.*" And not yet can I understand that "I."

OH, my Lord God, the Holy Scriptures are not so easily understood, even when one reads them diligently. Let us learn well these three words, and ever remain learners before them: to love, fear, and trust God.

BEFORE a man can truly understand the first word in Genesis, "*In* the *beginning* God created *the heavens and the earth,*" he dies. If he lived a thousand years he would not learn those words through and through.

MY best and Christian counsel is, that all should draw from this spring or well-head; that is, should read the Bible diligently. For he who is well grounded and exercised in the text will be a good and perfect theologian; since one saying or text from the Bible is better than many glosses and commentaries, which are not strong and sound, and do not stand the enemy's thrust.

THE Bible is a very large, wide forest, wherein stand many trees, of all kinds, from which we can gather many kinds of fruits. For in the Bible we have rich consolation, doctrine, instruction, exhortation, warning, promises, and threatenings. But in all this forest there is not a tree which I have not shaken, and broken off at least a pair of apples or pears from it.

CABALA was good until Christ; but now that Christ has come, and His grave stands open, all that is over. Our fanatics say that much is still dark in the Holy Scriptures, and not yet manifest. That is false, and not true; for the sepulchre is open, and Christ has come forth into the light. Therefore, whosoever knows Christ truly is a master in the Holy Scriptures, and remains a master.

IN this Book thou findest the swaddling-clothes, and the manger wherein Christ is laid. Thither the angels directed the shepherds. These swaddling-clothes may indeed be poor and little; but precious is Christ, the treasure laid therein.

ONCE when Jeit Dietrich said to the Doctor, in reference to heresies, "It would be better to pray not to be learned in the Holy Scriptures than to be learned in them," Doctor Luther answered, "No, no! we might as well pray that there should be no gold in the world, or no sun in the world; because without the sun many crimes could not be committed.

It is an abominable slander against the Holy Scriptures, and against all Christendom, to say that the Holy Scriptures are obscure. There never was written on earth a clearer book than the Holy Scriptures; compared with all other books, it is as the sun to all other light.

Let none tempt you away from the Scriptures. For if you step out of these you are lost; your enemies lead you whither they will. But if you keep to them you have overcome, and will heed their raging no more than the rock heeds the waves and billows of the sea.

Only be certain and doubt not that nothing is clearer than the sun, that is, the Scriptures. If a cloud glides before them, behind them is nothing but the same clear sun. So, if there is a dark saying in the Scriptures, doubt not; behind it, most surely, is shining the same truth which in other places is clear; and let him who cannot pierce the dark, keep to what is clear.

THE Word of God is a light which shines in darkness, brighter than the sun at mid-day. For in death not only is the light of this material sun extinguished, but even of reason with all her wisdom. But there, with all faithfulness, the Word of God still shines, an eternal sun, which faith only sees, and follows on into the clear Eternal Life.

I HAVE often said that from the beginning I have prayed the Lord that He would send me neither dream, nor vision, nor angel. But I have entreated also, with earnest prayer, that He would give me the true and sure understanding of the Holy Scriptures.

"AH, if I were only a good poet," he sighed, "I would fain write a costly Carmen, Song, or Poem, concerning the use, power, and fruitfulness of the Divine Word."

HE said, "You have now the Bible in German. Now I will cease from my labors. You have what you want. Only see to it, and use it after my death. It has cost me labor enough. What an unspeakable gift it is that God speaks to us."

IN the evening, bear something of sacred words with thee in thy heart to bed; chewing the cud of which, like a clean ruminant animal, thou mayst sweetly fall asleep.

But let it not be much in quantity; rather little, well pondered and understood; so that rising in the morning thou mayst find ready for thee the relics of last night's feast.

For in all study of the Sacred Scriptures we should despair of our own wit and labor, and seek understanding with fear and humility from God. At the close, and often during the reading, lift up the eyes of thy heart, and of thy body, to Christ, with a brief sigh imploring His grace, saying and thinking, " Grant, Lord, that I may rightly understand these things ; yet more, that I may do them. Behold, Lord Jesus, if this study be not to Thy glory, let me not understand a syllable. But give to me whatever shall seem to Thee for Thy glory in me a sinner."

SAINT JOHN the Evangelist speaks majestically, with very simple words ; as when he says, "*In the beginning was the Word.*"

See with what simple words he describes God the Creator, and all the creatures ; as with a flash of lightning.

If a philosopher and man of learning had undertaken to write of such things, how would he have gone round about with wondrous, swelling, high-sounding words, magnificent but obscure, *de ente et essentia*, of self-existence, and divine and heavenly powers, so that one could have understood nothing. Never were simpler words ; yet under such simplicity he says all.

Every word in him is worth an hundredweight ; as when he writes, " He came into a city of Samaria called Sychar, and spoke with a woman ; " and, " the Father honoreth the Son."

They are indeed, in appearance, slumbering words ; but when one wakes them up, and unveils them, and earnestly meditates on them, they are found indeed worthy.

UNDER the papacy they were constantly making pilgrimages to the shrines of the Saints; to Rome, Jerusalem, St. Iago de Compostella, in order to make satisfaction for sins; but now we may make true Christian pilgrimages, in faith, which will please God; that is, if we diligently read the Prophets, Psalms, Evangelists. Thus shall we make journeys, not through the earthly cities of the saints, but in our thoughts and hearts to God Himself; thus shall we make pilgrimages to the true Promised Land, and Paradise of Eternal Life.

II.

SPECIAL GRACES.

Love, Humility, Forbearance, Gentleness, Goodness.

Love.

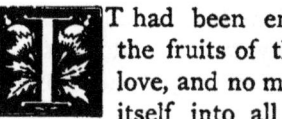

IT had been enough (in enumerating the fruits of the Spirit) to have said love, and no more; for love expandeth itself into all the fruits of the Spirit, when he saith, "Love is patient, courteous," &c.

Our love to our neighbors should be like a pure, chaste love between bride and bridegroom, by which all infirmities are veiled, covered, and made the best of, and only virtues looked at.

The law of Christ is the law of love. And to love is not merely to wish well one to another, but to bear one another's burdens, that is, to bear those things which are grievous unto thee, and which thou wouldst not willingly bear. Therefore

Christians must have strong shoulders and powerful bones, that they may bear flesh, that is to say, the weakness of their brethren; for Paul says that they have burdens and troubles. Love is mild, patient, courteous.

How Luther bore the Burdens of others.

WHEN Doctor Sebald and his wife both died of the plague, and Dr. Martin Luther took their children home to his own house, many blamed him and said he was tempting God. "Ah!" he said, "I had fine masters who would have taught me what it is to tempt God."

Joy.

THIS is the Voice of the Bridegroom and the Bride; that is to say, sweet cogitations of Christ, wholesome exhortation, pleasant songs and psalms, praises and thanksgivings.

God loveth not heaviness and doubtfulness of spirit; He hateth discomforting doctrine, heavy and sorrowful cogitations, and loveth cheerful hearts.

Joy and Fear.

DAVID says, "*Serve the Lord with fear, and rejoice before Him with trembling.*" Let some one make this rhyme for me: "to rejoice" and "to fear."

My little son Hans can do this with me, but I cannot do it with God. For when I sit and write, or do anything, he sings a little song to me the while; and if he makes it too loud, and I tell him so, then he still sings on, but makes it softer, crowing on with a sweet little subdued voice, slyly watching me all the time. So would God have it with us, that we should be always rejoicing, yet with fear and reverence before Him.

Grace and Peace.

THESE two words, grace and peace, do contain in them the whole sum of Christianity. Grace containeth the remission of sins; peace, a quiet and joyful conscience.

When the grace and peace of God are in the heart, then is man strong, so that he can neither be cast down by adversity, nor puffed up by prosperity; but walketh on evenly, and keepeth the highway, and is able to bear and overcome all troubles, yea, even death itself; for in spirit he walketh in the paradise of grace and peace.

Humility.

LEARN OF ME.

NO one ever made himself so low and little as Christ, so that He alone has the right to say, "Learn of Me, for I am meek and lowly in heart;" words which no Saint can venture to utter, nor ever more claim to himself the mastership in meekness and lowliness. All together they abide forever scholars under this Master.

The whole Gospel is nothing more than the history of this lowliest "Son of God," and of His humiliation.

BY His washing of the disciples' feet, the Lord Christ would show us that the kingdom which He was establishing should not be an outward, worldly kingdom, wherein there is respect of persons, one greater and higher than another, as in Moses' kingdom; but a kingdom wherein one should serve another by humility. "The greatest among you shall be as the youngest; and he that is chief among you as he that doth serve."

No man, if he were the gentlest and kindest in the world, could have such a gentle bearing as Christ had; for Christ is the Lamb of God, who beareth the sin of the world.

The Gentleness of Christ.

THERE is a legend of St. Peter, that he had always by him a cloth wherewith he wiped his eyes, which were often red with weeping. (And I can well believe it!) When he was asked why he wept, he said, "When he recalled that most sweet gentleness of Christ with His apostles, he could not restrain his tears." Christ must indeed have been perfect in kindness and tenderness. And even so and even such is he now daily with us, but we perceive it not.

The Silence of Christ.

CHRIST refrained from preaching and teaching until His thirtieth year, ever keeping silence, and suffering Himself not to be seen or heard in public. Throughout those years, what great and manifold impieties, idolatries, false religions, blasphemies, heresies, and schisms must He have seen. Yet He could refrain Himself until He was called to the office of the Prophet. This is much to be wondered at.

Luther Nothing in Himself.

MANY believe for my sake. But those only believe rightly who would remain steadfast in their faith, if they heard (which God forbid) that I had denied and apostatized. These believe not in Luther, but in Christ. The Word possesses them, and they possess the Word. Luther they can let go, be he a saint or a villain. God can speak as well through Balaam as through Isaiah, through Caiaphas as through Peter. Yea, He can speak by an ass.

I myself know nothing of Luther; will know nothing of him. I preach nothing of him; only of Christ. The devil may take Luther (if he can). If he leave Christ in peace, it will be well with us too.

So let us pray, before all things, that God may make His dear Child Jesus great in our hearts, from day to day, that with all eagerness and joy we may praise, bless, and confess *Him* before all.

Our God is the God of the low and the lowly. Power becomes strong in weakness; if we were not weak, we should be proud. It is only in weakness He can show His strength.

Humility the Secret of Unity.

TO MICHAEL DRESSEL AND THE AUGUSTINIAN CHAPTER AT NEUSTADT, 1516, 25 SEPTEMBER.

I HEAR with grief that though living in one house, you are living without peace and unity, neither are you of one heart and mind in the Lord. This miserable and useless way of living comes either from the weakness of your humility —for where humility is, there is peace—or from your and my fault, in that we do not entreat before the Lord who made us, that He will direct our way in His sight, and lead us in His righteousness. He errs, errs, errs, who by his own counsel presumes to direct himself, much more others. With humble prayer and devoted affection must we seek this from God.

There is peril in a life without peace, for it is without Christ, and is rather death than life.

ALL the works of God are embraced in the Magnificat. If a thing exalts itself, it is nothing; and again, when it is at the lowest and lowliest, it is once more exalted. If the weak in faith did not belong to Christ, what would have become of the Apostles, whom the Lord, even after His resurrection, often had to rebuke for their unbelief.

Bearing one Another's Burdens.
Forgive because forgiven.
TO GEORGE SPENLEIN—1516.

FOR the rest, about which thy soul is concerned, I desire to know whether, wearied out with her own righteousness, she is learning to breathe and trust in the righteousness of Christ. For in this our age, this temptation to presumption waxes hot in many, and chiefly in those who are struggling with their whole might to be just and good.

Ignorant of the righteousness of God, which in Christ is freely and most generously bestowed upon us, they seek in themselves to do such good works that at last they may have confidence in standing before God, as if adorned with virtues and merits; which is impossible to be done.

When thou wert with us thou wert of this opinion, and in this error, and I also. But now I contend against this error; not yet, however, have I overcome.

Therefore, my good brother, learn Christ, and Him crucified; learn to sing to Him, and despairing of thyself, to say to Him "Thou, Lord Jesus, art my righteousness, but I am Thy son. Thou hast taken on Thee what is mine, and Thou hast given to me what is Thine. Thou hast taken what Thou wast not, and given to me what I was not."

Take heed lest thou aspire to such a purity as not to seem to thyself a sinner. For Christ dwells only in sinners. For this cause did He descend from heaven, where He dwells in the just, that He might also dwell in sinners.

Ruminate on that love of His, and thou shalt be conscious of most sweet consolation in thy soul.

For if by our labors and afflictions it is possible for us to reach quiet of conscience, for what did He die? Therefore, nowhere save in Him, by a confiding self-despair, wilt thou find peace; whilst thou learnest of Him, that as He has taken thee on Himself, and made thy sins His, so also has He made His righteousness thine.

If thou firmly believest this, as thou shouldst (and he who believes not is accursed), then do thou also take on thee thy undisciplined and erring brethren, and patiently bear with them, making their sins thine own. And if thou hast anything good, let it be theirs. So teaches the apostle: "*Receive ye one another, as Christ also received us, to the glory of God.*" And again, "*Let this mind be in you, which was also in Christ Jesus, who being in the form of God, emptied Himself.*" So also thou, if thou seemest to thyself better than they, think it not robbery, or something meant for thyself alone, but "empty thyself," and forget what thou art, and be as one of them, that thou mayest sustain them.

For miserable is that righteousness, which by comparison deeming others worse, will not bear with them, but meditates to fly and desert them, when by patience and prayer while present with them it might be profitable to them. This is to hide the Master's talent, and not give it, as due, to the usurers.

Therefore, if thou art a lily and a rose of Christ, since thine abode must be among thorns, seek and strive with a single heart for the welfare of others, lest by impatience and rash judgment, or by hidden pride, thou thyself become a thorn.

The kingdom of Christ is in the midst of His enemies, as saith the Psalm. Dost thou, then, image to thyself that thine shall be in the midst of friends?

Thus, whatever thou lackest, prostrate before the Lord Jesus, ask for it. He Himself will teach thee all things. Consider only what He has done for thee, and for all, that thou also mayest learn what is due from thee to others.

If He had willed to live only amongst the good, and to die for friends, for whom, I ask, would He have died, or with whom would He have lived?

Thus do, my brother, and pray for me, and the Lord be with thee.

WITTENBERG, 1516.

THY BROTHER, MARTIN LUTHER, AUGUSTINIAN.

To the People of Wittenberg.
ON BEARING WITH THE WEAK.

CHRIST has borne our impotence in life and death. As Christ has done for us, we should do for our neighbor. He has borne our infirmities; so should we bear our neighbor's infirmities.

They have brought in these innovations in trivial things, and let faith and love go.

We have many weak brothers and sisters who dwell around us. These also must we take with us to heaven.

If Duke George and many others are angry and enraged with us, let us bear with them. It is possible that they may become better men than we are.

In these free things, we must nowhere insist; only, if our enemies insist on them as necessary things, we must resist.

Mark this emblem. The sun has light and heat. This light no kaiser nor king can quench. So also no one can quench the Word. But the heat we can flee, and go into the shade. Thus does Love, yielding to her neighbor, whenever needful.

The Incarnation the Bond between Men.
1521.

GOD has become man; nevermore, therefore, should we be enemies to any man.

We should be ready to lay down life for each other. Who would hate or injure the image in body and soul of Him who is thy God?

Those who wrong us still our Neighbors.

EVERY man is my neighbor, who although he hath done me some wrong, or hurt me by any manner of way; yet notwithstanding, he hath not put off the nature of man, or ceased to be flesh and blood, and the creature of God most like unto myself. Briefly, he ceaseth not to be my neighbor. As long, then, as the nature of man remaineth, so long remaineth the commandment of love, which requireth at my hand that I should not despise mine own flesh, nor render evil for evil; but overcome evil with good, else shall love never be as Paul describeth it.

GOD forgives sins of pure grace for Christ's sake; but we must not abuse His grace and forgiveness. Our Lord God has given us many signs that sins shall be forgiven us, namely, the preaching of the Gospel, Baptism, the Sacrament, and the Holy Spirit in our heart.

Now, it is also needful that we give a sign to show that we have received forgiveness of sins. This sign is, that each of us forgive his brother his trespasses. Although, indeed, between God's forgiveness and ours there is no comparison. What are the hundred pence to the ten thousand talents?

But to this brotherly forgiveness it is essential that the brother whom I am to forgive should confess his sins ; for sin which is not confessed, I cannot forgive. If my brother continues to wrong me, I must indeed suffer it, but I cannot forgive it, because he will not confess it.

Care for the Fallen.

TAKE care of this fallen brother of thine, yea, of ours. Nor do thou, averted from pity, abandon him who, subverted by impiety, abandoned thee. Let it not distress thee that ye suffer offence. To bear one another's burdens is that to which we are all called, baptized, ordained. For such has Christ been to us, such He is, such He will be forever; as it is written, "*Thou art a Priest forever.*"

Hope for the Fallen.—1516.

NO man hath so grievously fallen at any time, but he may rise again. And on the other hand, no man taketh so fast footing but he may fall. If Peter fell, I may likewise fall. If he rose again, I may also rise again.

A Child helping a Veteran.

GO to thy brother in hours of temptation. One alone is too weak to encounter the tempter. I am often glad of having even a child to speak to. This is so, in order that we may not glorify ourselves. Therefore at times I need and find help from one who has not as much theology in his whole person as I have in one finger, that I may learn what that meaneth, "*My strength is made perfect in weakness.*"

OFTEN when I have lain under temptation, and have been in anguish, Philip Melanchthon, or Dr. Pommer, or my own wife has comforted me with the Word of God, so that I came thereby into peace, and felt "God says this," because my brother said it.

I UNDERSTAND now that St. Paul was at times weak in faith, and when he went to Rome he was comforted when he saw that the brethren came to meet him.

Yielding for Peace' sake.

IF two goats meet each other on a narrow path above a river, what will they do? They cannot turn back; they cannot pass each other; if they were to butt at each other, both would fall into the water and be drowned. What then will they do? Nature has taught them, one to lie down, and let the other pass over it. Thus both are unhurt.

So should one man do to another; let himself be trodden under foot rather than quarrel and contend.

Toleration of Differences.

BY the Word alone I condemn. Let him who believes, believe and follow. Let him who believes not, not believe, and be dismissed. No man is to be constrained to faith and the things of faith, but to be drawn by the Word, that believing willingly, he may come spontaneously

Cease to contend by violence for the Gospel. By the Word the world is overcome. By the Word the Church is preserved, and by the Word she is restored.

CHRISTIAN freedom is no trifle, although it may concern a trifle.

I KNOW, I know it must be that offences come; neither is it a miracle for man to fall. The miracle is for man to rise again and stand upright. Peter fell that he might know himself to be a man. To-day also the cedars of Lebanon fall, whose tops touch the heavens. Nay (which surpasses all wonders), an angel fell in heaven, and Adam in Paradise.

What wonder then if a reed is shaken with the wind, and the smoking flax is quenched? The Lord Jesus teach thee, and work with thee, and finish the good work.

Thankfulness.

How God gives.

IF God refused us for a time the use of His creatures; if He once withheld the sun from shining, at another time imprisoned the air, or again dried up the waters, or quenched the fire, then we would indeed eagerly give all our money, and everything we possessed, to have once more the use of these creatures.

But because He lavishes His gifts and riches on us so freely and so abundantly, we claim them as a right. Thus the unspeakably great abundance of His countless benefits hinders and darkens our faith.

Constancy of God's Gifts leading to Ingratitude.

GOD gives sun and moon and stars and elements, fire and water, air and earth, and all creatures, body and soul, and all kinds of nourishment, in fruits, grain, corn, wine, and all that is needful and useful to preserve his temporal life.

And, besides, He gives us His good Word; yes, Himself.

What return is rendered to Him? Nothing else, but that He is blasphemed, and set at naught; yea, His dear Son grievously scorned, mocked, and hung on the cross; and His servants plagued, hunted down, and slain. This is our gratitude to Him for having created, redeemed, nourished, and preserved us.

IF God were to say to the Pope, the Emperor, kings, princes, bishops, doctors, rich merchants, burghers, and farmers, "Thou shalt die this very day, unless thou give Me a hundred thousand florins," every one would say, "Yes, with all my heart, if I may only live."

But now we are such thankless creatures, that we scarce sing Him a *Deo gratias* for the many and great benefits which we daily receive abundantly from His pure goodness and mercy.

Nevertheless, the gracious Father is not estranged by this, but is ever doing us good. If He stinted his gifts, instead of lavishing and showering them on us, we should thank Him more. For instance: if we were all born with one leg or foot, and only in our seventh year received the second leg; at fourteen one hand, at twenty a second, we might recognize more the worth of the gifts for a time withheld, and be more thankful.

WE are so shamefully perverse that we are unthankful for our present gifts and goods, and only think of little deficiencies. Let every one go home and count the gifts which he has; he will find far more gifts than deficiencies; and let him thank God for them.

To be used with Thanksgiving.

WHEN grapes, nuts, peaches, etc., were set on the table after the meal, and all were enjoying them, he said: "What does our Lord God on high, in heaven, say to our sitting here consuming His gifts? Verily for this purpose He created them, that we should use them; and He asks nothing from us but that we should acknowledge they are His gifts, and enjoy them with thanksgiving."

Two Sacrifices.

THE Scriptures point out two sacrifices which are well-pleasing to God. The first they call the sacrifice of praise, when we teach or hear God's Word with faith, and confess and spread it, and thank Him from our hearts for all the unspeakable gifts so richly given us in Christ. "He who offereth praise, he honoreth Me."

The other sacrifice is when an agonized, troubled heart takes refuge with God, seeks help from Him, and patiently waits for it. "The sacrifices of God are a troubled spirit. A broken and a contrite heart, O God, Thou wilt not despise."

The Church a Choir of Praise.

GOD has created all creatures, and nourishes and preserves them freely, out of pure goodness. But the little flock, dear Christendom, says Him a *Deo Gratias* for it.

On Giving and Communicating.

EVERY Christian has the priest's office, and does priestly work.

LET us be liberal and bountiful towards all men, and that without weariness. For it is an easy thing for a man to do good once or twice, but to continue, and not to be discouraged through the ingratitude and perverseness of those to whom he hath done good, that is very hard. Therefore he doth not only exhort us to do good, but also not to be weary in doing good. And to persuade us he addeth: "For in due season we shall reap if we faint not." As if he said, "Wait and look for the eternal harvest that is to come, and then no ingratitude or perverse dealing of men shall be able to pluck you away from well-doing; for in the harvest-time ye shall receive most plentiful increase and fruit of your seed." Thus, with most sweet words, he exhorteth the faithful to the doing of good works.

Date and Dabitur.

THERE was once a convent, which while it gave freely was rich, but when it became weary of giving it grew poor. Now, once upon a time one came to this convent and asked an alms, but they refused him. Then the beggar inquired why they would not give anything to him for God's sake? The porter replied, "We are poor." Thereupon the beggar said, "The cause of your poverty is, that once you had two brothers in the convent, but one of these ye have cast out, and the other has secretly crept after him, and is gone too. For when Brother *Date* is set at naught, then *Brother Dabitur* also departs.

Hoping for Nothing again.

A PERSON was once excusing himself by saying "he would gladly help and serve people, and do them good, but their ingratitude repelled him."

Then Dr. Martin Luther said, "Benefits and kindnesses should be conferred secretly, not with a view to fame; quietly and without seeking our own enjoyment, for God's sake, and for our neighbor's good."

THERE are three kinds of alms: first, that we give something towards the maintenance of the office of the preacher. Secondly, to relieve our poor friends and kindred. Thirdly, to help strangers, and those who live near us, or any who need our aid, and cannot live without the help of others.

THE noble Word brings naturally with it a burning hunger and an insatiable thirst, so that we cannot be satisfied even if thousands believe in it, but still long that no human creature may lack it.

Such a thirst suffers us not to rest, but impels us to speak (as David says, "I believed, therefore have I spoken." And St. Paul, "We having received the same spirit of faith, therefore we also speak"), until we would press the whole world to our hearts, and incorporate every one with us, and make, if possible, one Bread and one Body of all.

But not only does this thirst fall short of its longings; men still it with gall and vinegar, as with Christ on the cross.

Such a thirst had St. Paul when he wished that "every one were even as he, except these bonds;" when he wished to be "banished from Christ for his brethren's sake."

Such a thirst for the salvation of your brethren have ye now received, sure token of a faith sound at the root. What remains then but that ye also must await the vinegar and the gall? that is, calumny, shame, persecution, as the reward of this your Christian speaking.

How Luther gave.

TO HIS WIFE, ON A SERVANT LEAVING THEIR SERVICE.

SINCE Johannes is going away, I will do all I can that he may leave me well cared for. For thou knowest how faithfully and diligently he has served, and truly demeaned himself humbly, according to the Gospel, and has done and suffered all things.

Therefore think how often we have given gifts to good-for-nothing people, and to ungrateful students, on whom all was wasted; so look around thee now, and see that such a good fellow lacks nothing; for thou knowest it will be well spent and pleasing to God.

I know well there is but little to spare; but I would gladly give him ten florins if I had them. Less than five florins thou must not give him, for he has no stock of clothes. What thou canst give more, give, I pray thee. The common fund might present something for my sake to such a servant of mine, seeing that I have to keep my servants at my own cost, for the service and use of their church. But as they will. At all events be thou sure not to fail, as long as there is a silver tankard left. Think how thou canst provide it. God will surely give us more; that I know.

AGAIN, "To him who gives willingly it shall be given." Therefore, dear Käthe, when we have no more money, we must give the silver tankards.

DOCTOR MARTIN LUTHER went once, with Dr. Jonas, Master Veit Dietrich, and others of his guests, to walk in the little town of Tessen. There Doctor Martin Luther gave alms to the poor. Then Dr. Jonas also gave something, and said, "Who knows when God will repay me?" Thereupon Dr. Martin Luther said, laughing, "Just as if God had not first given it to you. Freely and simply should we give, from mere love, willingly."

Luther's Theology in his Seal.
TO LAZARUS SPENGLER.

SINCE you wish to know about the device for my seal, I will send you my first thoughts, which I would have my seal express, as a sign and token of my theology.

First, there shall be a cross, black, in a heart which shall have its natural color, that thereby I may remind myself that faith in the Crucified saves us. For if a man believes from the heart he is justified.

But although it is a *black cross*, because it mortifies, and must also cause pain, yet it leaves the heart its own color; that is, destroying not its nature; not killing, but preserving alive. For the just shall live by faith, but by the faith of the Crucified.

Moreover, this heart shall be set in the midst of a white rose, to show that faith gives joy, consolation, and peace, and sets the heart as in a white festive rose. Yet not as the world gives peace and joy; therefore shall the rose be white, and not red. For white is the color of angels and of spirits.

The rose is set in a sky-blue field; because such joy in the spirit and in faith is a beginning of the heavenly future joy—is indeed enfolded therein, and embraced by hope, but not yet manifest.

And in this field shall be a golden ring, because this blessedness endures eternally in heaven, and has no end, and is precious above all joy and all riches, as gold is the highest and most precious of metals.

Christ, our dear Lord, be with your spirit until that life. Amen.

Part Third.

WORDS FOR THE HALTING-PLACES.

WORDS FOR THE HALT-ING-PLACES.

I.

THE VISIBLE CREATION.

GOD writes the Gospel, not in the Bible alone, but on trees, and flowers, and clouds, and stars.

Creation the Veil of God.

ALL creatures are merely shells, masks (Larven), behind which God hides Himself, and deals with us.

GOD dealeth not with us in this life face to face, but veiled in shadows from us. "Now, through a glass darkly; but then, face to face."

Therefore we cannot be without veils in this life. But in this wisdom is required, which can discern the veil from God Himself; which wisdom the world hath not.

The covetous man heareth, indeed, that "man liveth not by bread alone, but by every word that proceedeth out of the mouth of God;" he eateth the bread, but seeth not God in the bread, for he beholdeth only the veil, and outward show. So he doth with gold and other creatures, trusting to them as long as he has them; but when they leave him he despaireth.

GOD has set the type of marriage everywhere throughout the creation. Each creature seeks its perfection in another. The very heavens and earth picture it to us.

THAT marriage is marriage; the hand a hand; wealth, wealth—that all can understand; but to believe that the marriage state is God's order; the hand God's creature; good clothing and riches His gift—it is God's work when men understand this.

Miracles in Common Things.

WE foolish creatures cannot comprehend with our reason how it is that we speak with our mouths, and whence the word comes, so that the voice of one man sounds in so many thousand ears; neither can we comprehend how our eyes see, nor how the bread and wine are changed into blood and muscle; nor how, when we sleep, as to the body we are dead, and nevertheless we live. And yet we seek to climb above ourselves, and to speculate about the high majesty of God, when we do not understand what is happening every day around us.

REASON cannot understand nor grasp how it is that of a little kernel comes a tree; how of a little grain of corn, which corrupts in the earth and perishes, twenty or thirty grains should spring to life.

Therefore the world is full of God's miracles, which happen without ceasing. But because they are so countless and so manifold, and moreover so altogether common, as says St. Augustin, we do not regard them nor think of them.

Christ once fed five thousand men, not counting the women and children, with five loaves, and when they had all had enough, there remained over and above twelve baskets full. If such a miracle happened now, all the world would wonder.

But that God is daily, without ceasing, working great miracles, the fleshly heart sees and regards not; far less will it wonder and give thanks.

God the Lord gives daily water from the rocks; bread from the sand; wine, beer, butter, cheese, and vegetables of all kinds from the earth. But because He gives them lavishly, without ceasing, no one holds it to be a miracle.

The blind world, forgetting Him, thinks all comes by chance. But on the other hand those who love Him, whithersoever they turn their eyes, whether they look on the heavens or the earth, the air or the water, see pure, obvious miracles of God, whereat they rapturously rejoice, and cannot enough wonder; have gladness and delight therein, and praise the Creator, and know that He also has delight in them.

THE whole world is full of miracles, but our eyes must be pure, lest, because they are so common to us, they become dim.

IN brief, in all, even in the smallest creatures, yea, even in their least members, we see the almighty power and the great wonder-working of God. For what man, however powerful, wise, and holy he be, can out of a fig make a fig-tree, or even one other fig? or out of a cherry-stone a cherry-tree, or even understand how God does it?

NO man can think out, or truly understand what God has done, and still ceaselessly is doing. Nor, if we sweat blood for it, could we write three lines such as St. John has written.

THE growth of every seed is a work of creation.

GOD is constantly making visible things out of invisible, and would fain have us do the same. But we reverse His way, and must needs see and grasp a thing before we will believe it.

The Creatures God's Army.

ALL the creatures are God's Host or Army. I have purposely kept the word *Exercitus*, army, as it stands in the Hebrew, to defy the devil, who is forever striving with all his powers, and in all kinds of ways, to hinder all the creatures in accomplishing the work for which God created them.

Flowers.

THE world, since Adam's Fall, knows neither God her Creator, nor His creatures; lives a life poorer than that of the cattle, honors not God, nor glorifies Him. Ah, if Adam had not sinned, how man would have recognized God in all the creatures, would have praised and loved Him, so that even in the smallest flower he would have seen and contemplated God's almightiness, wisdom, and goodness.

For truly who can think to the bottom of this, how God creates out of the dry, dull earth so many flowers of such beautiful colors, and such sweet perfume, such as no painter nor apothecary can rival? From the common ground God is ever bringing forth flowers, golden, crimson, blue, brown, and of all colors. All this Adam and his like would have turned to God's glory, using all the creatures with thanksgiving. But we misuse them senselessly, just as a cow or any unreasonable brute tramples the choicest and fairest flowers and lilies beneath its feet.

A Green Tree more glorious than Gold.

IF Adam had not fallen, all the creatures had seemed such to us, that every tree and every blade of grass had been better and nobler than if it had been of gold. For in the true nature of things, if we will rightly consider, every green tree is far more glorious than if it were made of gold or silver.

The Sun.

DOCTOR MARTIN LUTHER said he had observed and taken notice that the sun for the two last days had risen as if with a bound of joy. "He rejoiceth as a hero to run a race." It is a beautiful work of God that we, fallen creatures, dare not gaze at nor fix our eyes upon.

In Paradise we could have gazed on the sun with open eyes, without pain or hindrance.

A Rose.

HE had a rose in his hand, and was admiring it as a fair and excellent work and creature of God; and he said, "If a man were able to make one rose, he would be worthy of an empire."

The Dew.

I HAD not known what a lovely thing the dew is, unless the Holy Scriptures had commended it, when God says, "I will give thee of the dew of heaven." Ah, the Creation is a beautiful thing. When we ought to be understanding it, we lisp and stammer, and say "cledo" for "credo," like the babes. The word is strong, but the heart lisps. But our Lord God knows well that we are but poor little children, if we would only acknowledge it.

We can never understand, save through the Son. This is the sum of His discourse, "Per Me, per Me, *per Me.*"

Birds.

SEE! Christ makes the birds our masters and teachers, so that a feeble sparrow, to our great and perpetual shame, stands in the Gospel as a doctor and preacher to the wisest of men.

TOWARDS evening, two little birds who were making a nest in the Doctor's garden came flying thither, but were now and then frightened by those who were walking there.

Then the Doctor said, "Ah, thou dear little bird, fly not from me. From my heart I wish thee well, if thou wouldst only believe it. Just in this way it is that we distrust our Lord, who nevertheless gives us nothing but good. Surely He will never harm us who has given His Son for us.

"See the little birds, how choice and pure their way of life is. They lay the eggs so daintily in the nest, and brood over them. Then the nestlings peep out.

"If we had never seen an egg, and one were brought us from Calicut, in what a rapture of wonder we should be about it!"

ONE evening when he saw a little bird perched on a tree, to roost there for the night, he said, "This little bird has had its supper, and now it is getting ready to go to sleep here, quite secure, and content, never troubling itself what its food will be, or where its lodging on the morrow. Like David, it 'abides under the shadow of the Almighty.' It sits on its little twig content, and lets God take care."

DOCTOR LUTHER said, "How gladsome are the little birds; sing so deliciously; hop from one branch to another! They have no anxious cares about any want or scarcity that may come; are so content in themselves; and sing with a glad heart their morning and their evening song. Well might we take off our hats to them and say, 'My dear sir Doctor, I must confess I have not acquired this art of which thou art a master! Thou sleepest all night in thy little nest, without any care ; in the morning thou risest again, art joyful and well off ; settest thyself on a tree and singest and praisest God ; seekest afterward thy daily food and findest it. Why cannot I, old fool that I am, do the same, when I have so much reason to do it?' Can the little bird leave its cares, and keep itself in such fulness of content, like a loving saint, having neither acre nor barn, neither larder nor cellar, yet singing and praising, joyful and satisfied, because it knows that it has One who cares for it? Why then cannot we do the same, laboring indeed the while, to till the field and gather the fruits, and garner them against our need?"

NO one can reckon how much it costs only to feed the birds, and even those which are of no use. I consider it costs more to maintain all the sparrows for one year than the king of France's revenues, with all his wealth, rents, and taxes. What shall we say, then, of the food of all the other birds, ravens, jackdaws, crows, finches, and the rest ?

SPARROWS are the smallest and the most dissolute of birds ; yet they have the greatest glory. All through the year they have the best days, and do the greatest mischief. In the winter they infest the granaries ; in the spring they devour the seed in the field ; in harvest-time they have enough ; in autumn grapes and fruits are their refection. Ergo digni sunt omni persecutione.

The World our Storehouse.

GOD'S power is great, who nourishes the whole world. It is a difficult article truly to grasp, "*I believe in God the Father.*" He has created a plentiful provision for us. All seas are our cellars; all forests our hunting-grounds; the earth is full of silver and gold and countless fruits, all created for our sake. The earth is our granary and our store-chamber.

It is God who feeds us, not money.

GOD knows all handicrafts, and exercises them in the most skilful way. For the stag, He makes a coat to cover him, which would not of itself wear out for nine hundred years. For the stag's feet He makes shoes which last longer than the owner. And the sun is His hearth-fire, at which the food of all the creatures is cooked.

I WONDER how our Lord God finds wood for so many uses throughout the whole wide world; as wood for building, for burning, for carpenters, for coopers and wheelwrights, for beams of chambers, window-sashes, oars, candlesticks, cups, buckets, etc.

In brief, wood is the most useful and needful thing in the world, which we could not do without.

Cattle preaching to us,

ONE day when Doctor Luther saw the cattle in the field going to pasture, he said, "There go our preachers; the carriers of our milk, butter, cheese, wool, who daily preach to us faith in God, that we should trust Him as our Father, that He will care for us and feed us.

Divers kinds of Beasts.

WILD beasts are beasts of the Law, for they live in fear and trembling. But tame animals are creatures of grace; they live securely with man.

Beauty of some Creatures—their Use.

IT does not follow that God has created all plants merely that they may furnish food for man and beast. Many things were created that we may praise God for them. The stars, of what use are they, save that they praise God their Creator?

The Stars.

THE science of the stars and of the revolutions of the heavens is the oldest science of all, which brought many others with it. The ancients, especially the Hebrews, gave earnest heed to the movements of the heavens, as God says to Abraham: "Consider the stars; canst thou count them?" Astronomy is a beautiful gift of God, as long as she keeps to her own sphere; but if she steps beyond it, and seeks to prophesy future things, as the Astrologers do, this is not to be encouraged. I have gone so far in Astrology that I believe it to be nothing.

The Music of the Spheres.

PYTHAGORAS says that the movements of the stars make a beautiful concert and harmony, according with each other; but that men through constant use are now weary of this. It is indeed so with us. We have so many beautiful creatures around us that we heed them not, for their abundance.

All Creatures working freely according to God's Law.

WHATEVER a thing is created for, it does without law and unconstrained. A tree brings forth fruit freely by nature, unconstrained. The sun shines by nature, whereto God has created it, unbidden and uncompelled. And all creatures do of free will what they ought to do. So also God Himself is ever doing good by His nature and character, freely.

Thanksgiving for a Thunderstorm.

"THAT is a beautiful storm," he said once, with thanksgiving, when thunder came with a fruitful rain, awakening and moistening earth and trees. "Thus Thou givest, unthankful and covetous as we are! That is a fruitful thunder; it has touched the earth and opened its treasure-house, so that gives forth a fragrant perfume, just as the prayer of good Christians gives forth fragrance to God."

May.

ONCE in beautiful weather in May, he said, "What a picture of the Resurrection! See how the trees are dressed for their bridal! How delightfully all is growing green! What a precious May! Ah, that we would only trust God! What will it be in the life beyond, if God can show us such great delights in this pilgrimage, and this troubled life!

Man, not Nature, the Dwelling-place of God.

HEAVEN and earth, with all castles of kings and emperors, could not make a dwelling-place for God, but in the man who keeps His Word, there He will dwell.

Isaiah calls the heavens His throne, and the earth His footstool, but not His abode. We may search long to find where God is, but we shall find Him in those who hear the Words of Christ.

For the Lord Christ saith, "If any man love Me, he will keep My words, and we will make our abode with him."

II.

THE HOLY SCRIPTURES.

Persons.

IF Adam had remained in his innocence, and had not transgressed God's law, he would not always have remained in the same state in Paradise.

What a fair, glorious creature man had been, adorned with all wisdom and knowledge! He would have had joy and pleasure from all creatures, and what fair, joyous changes and transformations there would have been in all things.

He would have been received into eternal joy and into heaven, not through death, but through transformation and translation into another life.

EVE, the dear, holy mother, had good hope of Cain; was persuaded (it seems) that he was the seed of the woman which was to bruise the head of the serpent.

But the dear mother was mistaken; she had not yet fathomed her misery—knew not that "what is born of flesh is flesh;" she erred as to the time when this Blessed Seed, conceived of the Holy Ghost, should be born to the world of the Virgin Mary.

Eve.

WHEN Eve, his only companion and dear wife, bore Cain to Adam, there must have been great rejoicing; so when Abel was born.

But a great and bitter grief and heart-sorrow must the murder of Abel have been; bitterer to Adam than his own fall, since thereby once more he and his Eve became hermits on the earth.

Ah! Adam must have been a sorrowful man; our sufferings are child's play to his suffering and heart-sorrow.

If, through God's grace, he had not been of so good and strong a nature, he with his Eve must soon have died of sorrow. But the promise of the Seed of the woman comforted them.

The Early Patriarchs.

IT were worth a world to have the legends of the Patriarchs who lived before the flood; to know how they lived and preached, and what they preached.

Our Lord God must have thought, "I will bury these legends beneath the flood, for those who come after will heed them little, and understand them less. I will keep them until they meet each other in the other life."

So the dear Fathers who came after the flood, Abraham, Isaac, Jacob, also the Prophets and Apostles, whom the devil did not leave unassailed in this life, will have comforted themselves with thinking of the long delay of the earlier Patriarchs, and will have said, "I have a short time to reckon on compared with those before the flood; few years wherein to spread God's Word, and to suffer my cross and pain. What is my time compared with the unspeakable toil and labor, anguish, suffering, and vexation of our dear fathers of old, who suffered and endured seven or eight hundred years, both from the devil and the world?"

Esau and Ishmael.

HE said, "The rejection and casting away was only temporal. For Esau's hatred to Jacob his brother lasted only for a time, not always. And I believe that Ishmael and Esau were saved; for many among those nations received the Word of God."

Job.

JOB had much temptation even from his own friends, who pressed hard on him; therefore it stands in the text that his friends were angry with him. He made answer to them, "I know that I am no adulterer, murderer, nor thief." When he said that, they were angry with him, and vexed him sore. He, however, suffered them to chatter on, and was silent.

Job is an example of God's goodness and mercy; for holy he indeed is, but in temptation he fell much, yet he was not forsaken, for he is rescued and delivered again by God's mercy.

Moses and Aaron.

WHEN God has something great to accomplish, He begins the work through one man, and afterwards gives other helps, as with Moses and Aaron.

Jephthah's Vow.

JEPHTHAH, although the Spirit had come upon him, made a foolish and superstitious vow, after he gained the victory, that he would sacrifice his own daughter. If there had been a godly and reasonable man present, he could have made him sensible of the folly of this vow, and have said, "Jephthah! thou shalt not slay thy daughter on account of thy foolish vow. For the law concerning vows must be interpreted according to justice and fitness, not according to the letter."

David.

THERE never was a man who suffered more than David. His life is a true tragedy. There is nothing like it among the Greeks.

We are all poor schoolboys compared with him; we have indeed the same spirit, but nowhere are such gifts as his were.

He was a great rhetorician. He could weave one subject into a vast web, with words, as in the Hundred and Nineteenth Psalm. He could be brief, and embrace all religion and doctrine in one Psalm, as in the Hundred and Tenth.

Elijah.

IT is a terrible history, that of Elijah, that such a holy man prayed that it should not rain for such a long time. He must have been very indignant, because he saw the teachers of the people slain, and good godly men hunted down and persecuted.

The Prophets.

HE was asked about the mode of revelation to the Prophets, who always say, "Thus saith the Lord," whether God had spoken personally to them or not.

He said, "They were very holy, spiritual, diligent men, who meditated earnestly on holy things. Therefore God spoke to them in their hearts and consciences, and the prophets received it as a sure revelation.

Pilate.

"PILATE is a better man than any of the princes of the Empire who are not Evangelical," said Dr. Martin Luther. "He kept firmly to the Roman rights and laws, affirming that he could not suffer an innocent man to be ruined and put to death, his cause unheard, convicted of no one evil deed. Therefore he tried all honorable methods to set Christ free. But when they spoke to him of the displeasure of Cæsar, he was carried away, and let the Roman laws and rights go. For he thought, 'It is only one man, poor and despised; no one will take his cause up; what harm can his death do me? It is better that one should die, than that the whole nation should be set against me.'"

Then Master Johann Mathesius said to Dr. Martin Luther, he had known two preachers who had hotly debated these two questions: why Pilate scourged Christ? and why he said, "What is truth?" For one said Pilate had done it from compassion; the other, from tyranny and scorn.

Dr. Martin Luther answered: "Pilate was a kindly man of the world, and he scourged Christ from compassion, that he might thereby quiet the insatiable rage and fury of the Jews. And by his saying to Christ, 'What is truth?' he gave to understand as much as this: 'Why wilt thou dispute about truth, in this wretched life here in the world? It is worth nothing; but thou wilt be thinking about wretched disputes, and questions of the jurists, or thou mightest be set free.'"

WHEN Pilate asked Him, "Art Thou the king of the Jews?"—"Yes," He said, "I am, but not such a king as Cæsar; else would my servants and soldiers fight for me, to set me free; but I am a king sent to preach the Glad Tidings, that I might bear witness to the Truth." "What!" said Pilate, "If thou art a king of that kind, and hast such a kingdom as this, consisting in the word and the truth, thou wilt do no harm to my kingdom." And Pilate doubtless thought, "Jesus is a good, simple, harmless man, who is talking about a kingdom which no one knows anything about. Probably he comes out of some forest or remote region, is a simple creature who knows nothing of the world, or its government."

Judas Iscariot.

"JUDAS," said Dr. Martin, "is as necessary among the Apostles as three of the other Apostles. He solves countless questions and arguments. For instance, when they cast at us that there are many false brethren, and bad, un-christian men amongst us." True! Judas also was an Apostle; and no doubt he conducted himself as a more prudent man of the world than the rest. No one detected anything amiss in him.

Grace does.

DOCTOR MARTIN said one evening when he was at Lochau: "Oh! how I should like to have been once with the Lord Christ when He was rejoicing!"

The Triumphal Entry.

THE entry of the Lord Christ into Jerusalem must have been indeed a poor, mean, and beggarly entry, for Christ the great and mighty King sits on a poor borrowed ass. For John clearly shows that such asses were meant for poor people, who might use them in their need without paying any hire. The garments which the disciples laid thereon were His saddle. Yet it was a wonderful entry, according to the prophecy of Zachariah.

For when He came from Bethany to Bethphage on the Mount of Olives, which must have been as near Jerusalem as the bridge over the Elbe is to this town (Wittenberg), after he had awakened Lazarus from the dead, and a great multitude of people went before and followed, shouting and exulting, He sent His disciples to fetch the ass, and would ride on it, that the prophecy might be fulfilled.

I hold, however, that Christ Himself did not bring forward the prophecy, but the Apostles and

Evangelists. Christ, meantime, preached and wept; but the people did Him honor, with olive and palm branches, which are signs of peace and victory.

The Personal Appearance of St. Paul.

ONCE Magister Veit Dietrich asked him, "What kind of a person, Herr Doctor, do you think St. Paul was?" The Doctor said, "I think Paul must have been an insignificant-looking person, with no presence; a poor, dry little man, like Master Philip."

Books of the Holy Scriptures.

THE first chapter of Genesis comprehends the whole Scriptures.

IN Deuteronomy God has placed the most beautiful rules and laws for the government of the world.

IN the Book of Judges the excellent heroes and deliverers sent by God are depicted, who began and carried on all their works in trust in God, according to the First Commandment.

THE Books of the Kings go a hundred thousand steps before him who wrote the Chronicles, for he only points out the substance and the most remarkable passages and histories, and passes by what is simple and small. Therefore more honor is to be given to the Book of the Kings than to the Chronicles.

ECCLESIASTES is a very good and pleasant Book, although it is a fragment; it wants boots and spurs, and rides in sandals, as I used when in the cloister. It has many a fine rule for domestic government. It is like a Talmud, compiled from many books, perhaps from the library of Ptolemy Euergetes in Egypt.

SO also the Proverbs of Solomon were collected by others from the mouth of the king, perhaps as he sate at table or elsewhere, and brought together.

The Psalms.

AS this sweet book of David continued to be sung in all our churches, and to be chanted over so many thousand times in these incessant rounds and forms of prayer,—even by this frigid use of the Psalms some small savor of life was diffused abroad among many that were of an honest and good heart; and from these words themselves only, those that feared God drank in some little sweetness of the breath of life, and some small taste of consolation, like the faint fragrance that is to be found in the air that is not far from a bed of roses. Their experience was like also unto a simple man passing through a flowery and sweet-smelling meadow, who, though he knew not the peculiar nature and properties of the herbs and flowers, yet found his senses regaled with the general fragrance.

IF all the greatest excellences and most choice experiences of all the true Saints should be gathered from the whole Church since it has existed, and should be condensed into the focus of one book—if God, I say, should permit any most spiritual and gifted man to form and concentrate such a book—such a book would be what the Book of Psalms is, or like unto it. For in the Book of Psalms we have not the life of one of the Saints only, but we have the experience of Christ Himself, the head of all the Saints.

So that you may truly call the Book of Psalms a little Bible. Be assured that the Holy Spirit Himself has written and handed down to us this Book of Psalms as a Liturgy, in the same way as a father would give a book to his children. He Himself has drawn up this manual for His disciples; having collected, as it were, the lives, groans, and experiences of many thousands, whose hearts He alone sees and knows.

ALL other histories and lives of the Saints, which describe their acts and works only, when compared to the Book of Psalms, set forth to us nothing more than dumb saints; and everything that is recorded of them is dull and lifeless. But in the Psalms, where the very expressions of those that prayed in faith are recorded, all things live, all things breathe, and living characters are set before us in the most lively colors.

THE Psalms record not the common and every-day expressions of the saints, but those ardent and pathetic utterances by which, in real earnest, and under the very pressure of temptations, and in the very wrestlings of their souls, they poured out their hearts like Jacob, not before man, but before God! The Psalms give us therefore not only the works and words of the Saints, but the very hidden treasure of their hearts' feelings, the very inmost sensations and motives of their souls. They give thee not only the outward David, but the inner David; and that more descriptively than he could do it himself, if he were to talk with you face to face.

There you may look into the hearts of the Saints, as into Paradise, or into the opened heaven; and may see, in the greatest variety, all the beautiful and flourishing flowers, or the most brilliant stars, as it were, of their upspringing affections towards God for His benefits and blessings.

THE Psalms have this peculiarity of excellence above all other books of description, that the Saints whose feelings and sensations are therein set forth did not speak to the wind, under those their exercises and conflicts, nor to an earthly friend, but unto and before God Himself, and in the sight of God. And it is this that above all things gives a seriousness and reality to the feelings; it is this that affects the very bones and marrow, when a creature feels itself speaking in the very sight and presence of its God.

THE Book of Psalms, therefore, as it contains these real feelings of the Saints, is a book so universally adapted and useful to all Christians, that whatever one that truly fears God may be suffering, or under what temptation soever he may be, he may find in the Psalms feelings and expressions exactly suited to his case, just as much so as if the Psalms had been indited and composed from his own personal experience.

IN a word, if you desire to see the Christian Church painted forth in a most beautiful picture and in the most lively and descriptive colors, then take the Psalms into thy hands; this will be as a clear universal mirror, which will represent to thee the whole Church in its true features; and if there be one that fears God, it will present to thee a picture of thyself; so that, according to the maxim of the philosopher of old, γνωθι σεαυτον, thou wilt by this book come to a true knowledge of thyself, and also of God and all creatures.

The Book of Job.

THE Book of Job is a very good book, written not for his sake only, but for the consolation of all troubled, assaulted, grieved, suffering hearts.

It vexed and pained him that things went so well with the ungodly. Therefore this must be a comfort to poor Christians who suffer and are persecuted, namely, that in the life beyond, God will give them such a great, glorious, and eternal inheritance, and here also will set a bound to their sufferings.

Job did not speak just as it stands written in his book, but he thought it; for it is not thus that people speak in conflict and temptation; but the fact and marrow of the thing was this.

It is just like an *argumentum Tabulæ*, as in a drama, in which various Persons are brought on, one speaking to or after another, as it is in his heart; thus the **Master has** described it; as Terence his comedies.

He intended to give an example of patience.

It is possible that Solomon wrote this, for it is almost his way of speaking, as in others of his books.

I hold it to have been a true history. This history of Job must have been ancient and well known in the days of Solomon, if indeed he undertook to narrate it, as if I undertook to write the history of Joseph, or of Rebecca.

The Hebrew poet and master who wrote this book, be he who he may, had himself seen and experienced such conflicts and temptations as he describes.

DANIEL and Isaiah are the two most excellent Prophets.

THE preaching of the Prophets is not given whole and entire, but their disciples and hearers took down from time to time one saying and another, and so put them together. Thus was the Bible preserved.

III.

THE FATHERS AND DOCTORS OF THE CHURCH.

THE ancient Fathers and Doctors, as Augustine, Hilary, Ambrose, Bonaventura, and others, should not be cast aside, but held in esteem and honor. For we see in them that the Church in their days believed in Jesus Christ, and believed as we do now.

St. Augustine was an excellent teacher. He taught faithfully of the grace of God.

Hilary and Augustine have written many beautiful things about the Holy Trinity, and about justification.

To Bernard Jesus is as dear as to any one in the world.

Of "St. John Huss the Martyr."

IN John Huss the Holy Ghost was very powerful, in that he was able to stand so joyfully and steadfastly for the Word of God, he alone against such great peoples and nations; Italy, Germany, Spain, France, England, assembled at the Council of Constance.

Against all this clamor he stood, and bore it, and was burned.

Rome would not suffer him to whisper in a corner, and is now constrained to suffer him to cry aloud through all the world, until Rome itself and the whole world are become too narrow for that cry, and nevertheless there is no end to it.

Legends of the Saints.

DR. MARTIN said once he wished much that the legends of the Saints could be wisely selected from. There was much to learn from some of them.

THE legend of St. Margaret is an ecclesiastical allegory and type of the Church. For the Church is the costly Margarita, the precious Pearl; Olybrius the tyrant is the world, which resists the Church, throws this precious Pearl Margaret into the dungeon, where she is tormented and vexed with many assaults from the devil, which she cannot escape until she grasps the Cross—that is, Christ. Thus the dragon is driven away and slain.

DOCTOR MARTIN preached about St. Christopher on his festival, and said that "his legend was not a history, but that the Greeks, as a wise and learned and gifted people, had imagined it to signify what a Christian should be, and how it would go with him. It is a beautiful Christian poem."

So, also (he said), is it with the legend of St. George and the Dragon.

IV.

HEROES.

GREAT men and heroes are especial gifts of God, men whom He gives and upholds, who carry on their work and calling, and do great deeds; not puffed up with empty imaginings or droning on with cold, sleepy thoughts; but especially stirred and driven by God thereto, they fulfil their course and work; as King Alexander gained for himself the Persian Empire, and afterwards Julius Cæsar the Roman Empire.

Thus also have the Prophets, St. Paul, and other great and noble men, done and fulfilled their work by the especial grace of God, as the Book of Judges shows, wherein we see how God gave great things with one man, and with him withdrew them.

Simplicity of True Heroes.

FRANK, open-hearted soldiers have few words—are modest, do not boast, do not talk much; for they have seen men. When they speak, the deed goes with the word, as with my Lord Bernard von Mila. In his manners he was like a maiden, right noble man that he was; he had much of the lion in his heart, but in words was gentle and unpretending.

Grace using, not destroying Nature.

GRACE does not altogether change nature, but uses it as it finds it. For instance, when a man who is kind and gentle by nature is turned to the faith, like Nicolas Hausmann, grace makes him a tender, gentle preacher; whilst of a man who is naturally given to anger, like Conrad Cordatus, it makes an earnest, serious preacher; whilst if another has a subtle and powerful understanding and wit, that also is used for the benefit of the people.

Princes whom Luther honored.
THE ELECTOR FREDERIC OF SAXONY.

THE Elector Frederic was a wise, understanding, able, and excellent prince, a great enemy to all pomp and pretence and hypocrisy. A pious, God-fearing, prudent prince, such as Duke Frederic, Elector of Saxony, was, is a great gift of God. He was a true father of the fatherland. With his officials, castellans, stewards, and servants he kept accurate accounts.

DUKE JOHN OF SAXONY.

THE wonderful steadfastness of the Elector John at the Diet of Augsburg was greatly to be praised. He said: "There are two ways: to deny God, or to deny the world. Let each man consider which is the best." It is a great miracle and grace of God that one Elector should have stood so firm against the rest, and also against the Emperor.

THE physicians say Duke John died of cramp. As infants are born without care, live without care, die without care; so will it seem to our dear prince Duke John at the Last Day, as if he had come in from the forest after the chase; he will not know what has happened to him. As Isaiah says, "The just is taken away; he shall enter into peace; they shall rest on their beds."

PHILIP, LANDGRAVE OF HESSE.

DOCTOR MARTIN LUTHER praised the Landgrave much, that he was a good, understanding, and merry-hearted prince, who kept good peace in his land, which was full of forests and rocks, so that the people could dwell securely therein, work and trade. For if any one was robbed and plundered, instantly he pursued the thieves and punished them, just as his father had done, who once restored three thousand florins to one who had been robbed of them; and when he discovered who had done it, razed his castle to the ground, the delinquent himself having fled. For he said it was for this they ruled, that the land might be kept pure.

The Landgrave is for his age an excellent prince, who suffers himself to be spoken to and counselled; soon yields to good counsel; and when he has decided, delays not long, but executes with diligence; therefore for these princely virtues he is feared by his adversaries. He has a Hessian head—cannot be idle; must have something to do; trusts and believes not lightly.

KAISER MAXIMILIAN.

ONCE when the king of Denmark had sent a solemn embassy to Kaiser Maximilian, and the Ambassador claimed such honor for his sovereign as to demand to give his message to the Emperor sitting, the Emperor, observing it, stood up to hear him, so that, for shame, the Ambassador had to stand also.

On the other hand, once, when another Ambassador, at the commencement of his address, lost his presence of mind and stopped short, the Emperor began to speak easily to him of other things, to give him time until he recovered.

Again, once, when an impudent beggar asked alms of the Kaiser, and called him " Brother, because they were both children of one fallen Adam," Kaiser Maximilian said to him, " See! there are two kreuzers. Go to the rest of thy brothers ; if they give thee as much, thou wilt be a richer man than I."

Tene mensuram et respice finem was Kaiser Maximilian's motto. A finer dictum than Kaiser Karl's *Plus ultra*.

The Love of their Subjects the true Treasure of Princes.

PHILIP MELANCHTHON said once to Doctor Martin Luther at table that "he had heard in his youth how, at a Diet, several princes had boasted of the excellences of their respective territories.

" The Duke of Saxony said he had silver under his mountains, and mines which yielded great revenues.

" The Count Palatine praised his good Rhenish wine.

" But Duke Eberhard of Würtemberg said, ' I am a poor prince, and cannot compare myself with either of your graces (Liebden) ; nevertheless, I have this treasure in my land, that were I riding anywhere therein, alone and unattended, I could find a night's lodging, safe and welcome, in the home of any of my subjects.'

"And all the princes held this to be the best treasure of all."

KAISER MAXIMILIAN said, "There were three kings in the world. He himself, the Emperor; the king of France, and the king of England. He was a king of kings; for when he required anything of his princes which pleased them they did it, and if not, they let it alone. The king of France was a king of asses, for all that he commanded of his people they had to do, like beasts of burden. But the king of England was a king of men; for what he required of them they did willingly, and held their prince dear, like obedient subjects.

V.

CHILDREN.

ON the last day of September Dr. Martin saw his little children sitting at the table, and he said:
"Christ says, ' *Verily I say unto you, except ye be converted and become as little children, ye shall not enter the kingdom of heaven.*' He affirms it with an oath (verily). O my God, surely Thou makest it all too simple; to lift children, such little foolish creatures, so high! How comes it that Thou hast bidden and taught thus, that a little simple child should be preferred before a sage? How can this consist with our Lord God's judgment and righteousness, which Paul exalts so high? Righteousness of God! Righteousness of God! Is this thy righteousness, that Thou castest out the prudent and receivest babes? The answer is, 'Believe God's Word and surrender thyself.' Our Lord God has purer thoughts than we men. He must prune and polish us, and

cut away great branches and boughs, ere He can make us such children and babes again.

"See what pure thoughts little children have; how they look at heaven and death without any doubting. They are as if in Paradise."

HIS little son once sat at the table and lisped and prattled about the life in heaven, and said what great joy there must be in heaven with eating, dancing, etc. There must be the greatest of all pleasures; the brooks flowing with pure milk, and cakes growing on the trees. Then Dr. Martin said, "The life of little children is the most blessed and the best of all, for they have no temporal cares, know nothing of the frightful, monstrous fanaticism in the Church, suffer no terror of death, nor of hell, have only pure thoughts and joyful speculations."

HE was once playing and having little games with his little daughter Lenichen, and he asked her, "Lenichen, what will the Holy Christ bring you this Christmas?" and then he added, "Little children have such choice thoughts of God, how He is in heaven, and is their own dear Father."

DOCTOR MARTIN, in the year 1538, on the 17th of August, heard that his children had been quarrelling with each other, and soon afterward had been reconciled. Then he said,

"My Lord God, how well this life and these plays of the little ones must please Thee! Indeed, all their sins are nothing but forgiveness of sins."

DOCTOR MARTIN was noticing one day how his little child of three years old was playing and prattling to himself, and he said, "This child is like one intoxicated; knows not that it lives; lives joyfully, without fear; springs and dances for joy."

ONCE when his infant son was brought to Dr. Martin, and he kissed and embraced it, he said, "My God, how dearly Adam must have loved Cain, the first-born human creature. And afterward he became a fratricide! O Adam, woe, woe to thee!"

DOCTOR MARTIN once would not suffer his son to appear before him for three days, nor would he take him again into favor until he had written, and humbled himself for his fault, and entreated forgiveness.

And when his mother, Dr. Jonas, and Dr. Teutleben pleaded for the boy, he said, "I would rather have a dead than an unworthy son. St. Paul said a bishop should be one that brought up his own children well, that others might take example thereby."

PARENTS are to be honored above all magistrates, for they are the fountain and source of the Fourth Commandment.

THE life and the faith of children is the best, for they have only the Word; and to it they hold fast, and simply give God the honor of believing that He is truthful, holding what He promises for certain.

ANOTHER time he took his infant son and said to him, "Thou art our Lord God's little babe (Närrchen), livest under His grace and the forgiveness of sins, not under the Law. Thou fearest not, feelest safe, and troublest thyself about nothing. With thee all is unspoiled and uncorrupted."

HIS little son Martin had a little dog with which he was playing. Once when his father saw it, he said, "This babe preaches the Word of God in word and deed, for God says, 'Have dominion over the cattle.' And the dog will suffer anything from the child."

WHEN it was told him that his little daughter of four years old often spoke with joyful confidence of Christ, of the dear angels, and of eternal joy in heaven, he once said to her, "Ah! dear child! if we only firmly believe it!" Thereupon the little maiden with anxious looks asked her father "If he did not believe it?" And Dr. Martin Luther observed, "The dear children live in innocence, know not of sin, live without any anger, avarice, or unbelief, and are therefore joyful and of a good conscience, fear no danger, be it of war, pestilence, or death. And what they hear of Christ and of the future life they believe simply, without any doubt, and speak joyfully about it. Therefore Christ earnestly appeals to us to follow their example. For the children really believe, and therefore Christ holds little children and their childlike ways dear."

MY little Magdalene and Hans pray effectually even for me and many Christians.

CHILDREN under seven years old have the most joyful dying. They have not yet learned the fear of death.

DOCTOR MARTIN LUTHER once blessed one of his little children in its aunt's arms, and said, "Go thy way, and be good. Money I shall not bequeath thee, but I shall leave thee a rich God. He will not forsake thee."

Children should be taught at Home.

PUBLIC sermons do little for children; they bring little from them, unless in the school and at home they are diligently examined as to what they have learned.

"WOMEN," he said, "are eloquent by nature, and are well skilled in rhetoric, in the art of persuading, which men have to learn and conquer with great pains."

"KÄTHE," he said to his wife, "you have a good husband who loves you. You are an empress." And of her he said he held her dearer than the kingdom of France, and the dukedom of Venice.

HE said once, "When women embrace the doctrine of the Gospel they are far stronger and more fervent in the faith, and hold it more firmly than men, as we see in the good Anastasia; and Magdalene's heart was more steadfast than Peter's.

Schools.

WHEN schools flourish, all flourishes, and the Church remains upright. Schools preserve the Church.

Printing.

PRINTING is *summum et postremum donum* through which God sends forth the Gospel. It is the last flicker of the flame before the extinguishing of the world. The world, thank God, is near its end. The holy Fathers who have fallen asleep would have desired to see this day of the unveiled Gospel.

VI.

MUSIC.

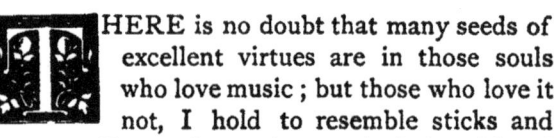

THERE is no doubt that many seeds of excellent virtues are in those souls who love music; but those who love it not, I hold to resemble sticks and stones. For we know that music is hateful and intolerable to the demons. And I fully deem, and am not ashamed to assert, that after Theology there is no art which can be compared to music. For she alone, after Theology, produces that which otherwise Theology alone can produce, a glad and quiet heart. Wherefore the devil, author of sad cares, and of crowds of disquiets, flies at the voice of music, as he flies at the word of Theology.

THE devil is a sad spirit, and makes men sad; therefore he cannot endure cheerfulness. That is why he flies as far as he can from music, remains not where there is singing, especially of hymns. Thus David softened Saul's temptation by his harp.

DOCTOR MARTIN said, in the year 1541, that music is a glorious and divine gift, which is altogether hostile to the devil, and many temptations and desponding cogitations may be driven away thereby, for the devil cannot endure music.

MUSICAL notes make the text living. They drive away the spirit of depression. Some of the kings, princes, and nobles must maintain musicians; for it becomes great potentates and rulers to preserve free, noble arts and laws.

MUSIC is the best refreshment of a troubled man, whereby his heart is again brought into peace, invigorated, and refreshed.

MUSIC is a discipline, and a mistress of order and good manners; she makes the people milder and gentler, more moral and more reasonable.

IN the year 1538, on the 17th of December, when Dr. Martin had the singers as his guests, and they sang beautifully lovely motets and pieces, he said with admiring wonder:

"If our Lord God has poured forth such gifts

in this poor fallen life, what will it be in that eternal life, where all will be the pleasantest and most perfect? Here we have only the beginnings."

MUSIC has always been dear to me. Whoever is capable of this art, is of a good kind, is capable of all things good. Music must be kept up in schools. A schoolmaster must be able to sing, otherwise I will not look at him. Nor should men be ordained preachers until they have been well tried and exercised in the school.

ONCE when a choice motet of Senfl's was sung, Dr. Martin admired and praised it much, and said, "I could not compose such a motet, if I were to strain myself to any extent to do it; and he on the other hand could not explain a Psalm as I can. Thus the gifts of the Spirit are manifold, as in the body there are many members. But no one is content with his gifts. Each member wishes to be the whole body, not one member."

ONCE, as they were singing the Passion, Dr. Martin listened attentively, and said, "Music is a precious, beautiful gift of God. Often it has so awakened and moved me, that I have been filled with the desire to preach."

MUSIC is a beautiful, glorious gift of God, and ranks next to Theology. The young should be exercised in this art, for it makes capable men.

SINGING is the best art and exercise. It has nothing to do with the world, is nothing before the tribunals, or in matters of strife. Singers are not anxious and careful but joyful, and with singing drive cares away.

DOCTOR MARTIN said once to a harper, "My friend, play me a song, as David did. I think, if David rose from the dead now, he would wonder to find how far we have advanced with music. It was never better than now."

WHEN David struck the harp it must have been like the Magnificat in the Eighth Tone, for David can scarcely have had a *Decachordum*.

HOW is it that on earthly things we have many a fine poem and carmen ; and on spiritual things such poor cold things ?

WHOEVER despises music, as all fanatics do, with him I am not content. For music is a gift of God, not of man. It drives away the devil and makes people joyful. Through music one forgets all anger, impurity, pride, and other vices. Next to Theology I give to music the highest place and honor. And we see how David and all the Saints have wrought their godly thoughts into verse, rhyme, and song, *quia pacis tempore regnat musica.*

Part Fourth.

WORDS FOR THE WOUNDED.

WORDS FOR THE WOUNDED.

I.

TRIAL OF VARIOUS KINDS.

Passio optima Actio.

NEVER do we do more and in a holier way than when we know not how much we do.

Never do we do worse than when we know what and how much we do; for it is impossible that we should not be pleased with ourselves. The stain of glory and ambition soils such works, so that our praise of God is no longer pure. *Ideo est passio optima actio.* Suffering is the best work.

The Cross.

THE Cross of Christ is divided throughout the whole world. To each his portion ever comes. Thou, therefore, cast not thy portion from thee, but rather take it to thee as a most sacred relic; and lay it up, not in a golden or silver shrine, but in a golden heart, a heart clothed in gentle charity.

For if the wood of the cross is so consecrated by contact with the flesh and blood of Christ, that it is held the choicest of relics, how much more are persecutions, sufferings, and the unjust hatred of men (whether of the just or the unjust), most sacred relics; sacred not by the touch of His flesh, but embraced, kissed, blessed, and to the utmost consecrated by the charity of His godlike will, and of His most loving heart, whereby the curse is transformed into blessing, and injury into justice, and suffering into glory, and the cross into joy.—1516.

LET no one lay on himself a cross, or desire a trial. But if one comes on him let him suffer it, and know absolutely that it shall be good and profitable to him.

IF tribulation takes all away from us, it still leaves God; for it can never take God away. Nay, indeed, it brings God to us.

The Peace of God under the Cross.

HEALTH and peace to thee, but not such as are manifest to the senses of men, but hidden under the cross, and passing all understanding in the Lord.

Thou seekest and cravest peace, but vainly.

For as the world giveth, seekest thou; not as Christ giveth.

Dost thou not know that God is wonderful in His people, and placeth His peace in the midst of no peace, that is, of all temptations? As it is said, "*Reign Thou in the midst of Thine enemies.*"

Not he, therefore, hath peace whom none troubleth; this is the peace of the world; but he whom all men and all things trouble, yet who beareth all these things quietly, with joy.

Thou sayest with Israel, "Peace, peace, and there is no peace." Say rather with Christ: The Cross, the Cross, and there is no cross. For the cross ceaseth to be the cross as soon as thou canst contentedly say, Crux benedicta, inter legna nullum tale,

> "Blessed Cross, in all earth's forests
> Grows no other wood like thine."

See, then, how faithfully the Lord is leading thee to true peace, who surroundeth thee with so many crosses.

It is called "the peace of God which passeth all understanding;" that is, which is not known by feeling or perception, or thinking. All our thinking cannot attain nor understand it; none but those who of free-will take up the Cross laid on them,—these, tried and troubled in all they feel and think and understand, afterward experience this peace. For all our feeling, all our labor, all our thinking He has estimated below this peace of His, and has affixed it to the Cross; that is, to many and disquieting troubles. Thus it is a peace above sense and all else that we picture and desire, indeed better far beyond all comparison than these. Seek, therefore, this peace of His, and thou shalt find. But thus shalt thou seek it best; not by seeking and choosing a peace according to thine own opinion and understanding, but by taking up thy troubles with joy, as sacred relics.—A. D. 1516.

Chastening—Entreating.

IF a father do sharply correct his son, it is as much as if he said, " My son, I pray thee to be a good child."

It seemeth indeed to be a correction, but if you regard the father's heart, it is a gentle and earnest beseeching.

Heaviness of Heart.

ST. PAUL confesseth that God had mercy on him, in that he restored Epaphroditus, so weak and near unto death, unto health again, lest he should have sorrow upon sorrow.

Therefore, besides outward temptations, it is evident that the Apostles also suffered great anguish, and heaviness, and fear.

Trial the Interpreter of Scripture.

VEXATIO DAT INTELLECTUM. Tribulation teaches; as saith Sirach, "He who is not tried, what does he know?"

None understand the Scriptures save those who prove them by the Cross.

Our Quære not always answered here.

GOD will give us all things in Christ, that He Himself may be ours, if we humble ourselves in true faith before Him.

But we will not, and go about with *Quære: Why* God does this or suffers that? For we also would play our part in the game.

The Quære answered hereafter.

WHEN Dr. Martin was once asked why God did many things of which no one could find out the reason; "Ah!" he said, "we have not power to understand all that God does. He wills not that we should know all He purposes. As He said to Peter, 'What I do thou knowest not now, but thou shalt know hereafter' (*in that joyful Day*). Then shall we first truly understand how faithfully and kindly God has meant with us, even through misfortune, anguish, and necessity. Meantime we must look with sure confidence to Him, that He will not suffer us to be really harmed in body or soul, but will deal with us so that, good or bad, all must work for the best."

Even as a Father the Son in whom He delighteth.

GOD deals not otherwise than a father with his son and his servant. The son he corrects and smites far oftener than the servant, but meantime He is gathering a treasure for him to inherit. But a bad, disobedient servant he does not smite with the rod; he drives him from the house, and gives him no inheritance.

Better anything from God than Silence.

"OH my God! punish far rather with pestilence, with all the terrible sicknesses on earth, with war, with anything rather than that Thou be silent to us."

Flying to God in Sorrow, not from Him.

IT must at last come to this, that we no longer fly from God as from an executioner. For if we fear and fly Him, *with whom shall we take refuge?* If we lose Him, all is lost.

Victory by Submission.

WHOEVER can earnestly from the heart humble himself before God, and acquiesce in His chastening, has already won the victory. Otherwise our Lord God would lose His

Godhead. He is merciful, gracious, patient, of great goodness, and His own prerogative and work it is to have pity on the wretched, to comfort the sorrowful, not to despise the anguished, smitten heart; to help them to right that suffer wrong, to give grace to the lowly.

REST IN THE LORD; WAIT PATIENTLY FOR HIM. In Hebrew (said Dr. Luther), be silent to God, and let Him mould thee. Keep still, and He will mould thee to the right shape.

David singing Psalms in Trial.

WHEN David could remedy an evil he did his utmost to that end; but when he knew of no counsel nor help against a thing, he had to exercise patience; and he made a song to God about it, sang it, and called on Him.

David had worse devils to contend against than we have, for he had such great revelations as cannot be had without great temptations. David made Psalms and sang them. We also, as well as we can, will make psalms, and sing them to the glory of our God, and in defiance of the devil and the world.

"WHEN I am pressed with thoughts," said Dr. Martin once, "about worldly or home cares, I take a Psalm, or a saying of Paul, and go to sleep on it."

THE holy Cross, temptation, and persecution teach the golden art ; but flesh and blood can never like them, would fain have peace and ease.

Our Lessons need to be learned over and over.

WHEN one trial is over, another soon comes, against which we have to arm ourselves. And when the second comes, we bear ourselves just as in the first, as if we had never been tried before, become grieved and distressed, and sink beneath it, are no more learned than before, although we have had experience before. We soon forget.

Thus the Evangelist rebukes us, saying, "And they understood not, neither remembered the miracle of the loaves."

But St. Paul exhorts us "not to be wearied or faint in our minds," when one trial follows, and one billow chases another, for thus our flesh is disciplined, for our good.

"The Order of Christ."

BARLEY has much to suffer from men. For it is cast into the earth, where it perishes. Then when it has sprung up and ripened it is cut and mown down. Afterward it is crushed and dried, and pressed, fermented, and brewed into beer.

Just such a martyr also is linen or flax. When it is ripe it is plucked, steeped in water, beaten, dried, hacked, spun, and woven into linen, which again is rent or worn out. Afterwards it is made into plasters for sores and used for binding up wounds. Then it becomes lint, and is laid under the stamping-machines in the paper-mill, and torn into small bits. From this they make paper for writing and printing.

These creatures, and many others like them, which are of great use to us, must thus suffer. So also must all good and godly Christians suffer much from the ungodly and wicked.

David, for instance, was a wonderfully gifted man, and he had to be ploughed and crushed. But such a man is dear to God.

Christ more compassionate than any Christian.

SCHLAINHAUFFEN complained of his trials, on the right hand and on the left. Dr. Luther said, "That the devil can do in a masterly way; otherwise he were no devil. Come to me, dear friend, to Philip, to Cordatus, and believe that we will surely comfort you with God's Word. But if you expect good from me, what may you expect from Christ, who died for you? Ah, if you would only look for good thus from Him, who is a thousand times better than me, or Philip, or Cordatus!"

A CHRISTIAN should be a joyful man. We must suffer many things from within and from without, both from the world and the devil. But let them pass; be of good cheer, call on God, and have patience. He is a help in need, will not leave thee comfortless and helpless, or suffer thee to be overwhelmed and ruined in trial. Trials are good and needful for us, that God's power may be the stronger in our weakness. See how faint-hearted the dear holy patriarchs, prophets, apostles were! What then could we poor, feeble little worms expect to be in such a godless world, when godliness, faith, and love are grown so cold, and well-nigh extinguished? Yet God upholds the Church in a wonderful way.

The Types set in this Life to be read in the Next.

ON the 8th of August, in the year 1538, Dr. Martin, and also his wife, lay sick of a fever. Then he said, "God has smitten me rather hard. I have also been impatient, because I am exhausted by so many and such severe illnesses. But God knows better what end it serves than we ourselves do. Our Lord God is like a printer, who sets the letters backward. We see and feel Him set the types, but here we cannot read them. When we are printed off yonder in the life to come, we shall read all clear and straightforward. Meantime we must have patience.

IT may be admitted that Purgatory works in this life, in its sphere. True Christians are cleansed and purged therein.

THE sicknesses of the heart are the true sicknesses, such as depression, temptations, etc. I am a very Lazarus, well exercised in such sickness as this.

WE who are baptized must endure and suffer both actively and passively from God, who creates and works all in us; and also from the devil and the world, who will torment and vex us.

ONCE when Master George Rörer's children lay ill, Dr. Martin said, "Our Lord God afflicts all His saints. They must all drink of that cup. He dealt thus even with Mary His mother. All dear to Him must learn to endure. Christians conquer when they suffer. When they resist they lose the day."

The Barley and Flax again.

WE must suffer. For as the barley from which beer is made, and the flax from which linen is made, must suffer much ere they are fit for use, and the end is attained for which they are sown, so must Christians suffer much, must be sown, torn (like flax), crushed and winnowed (like corn). For the slaying of the old Adam goes before the glorifying. If we are to be saved, and to come to glory, we must first die and be slain.

The Incarnation the greatest Consolation in Sorrow.

THIS highest benefit and mystery, that the Son of God condescends to become man and my brother, no power of eloquence can utter, no human thought can fully grasp.

He Himself so binds Himself, so unites Himself to me, with a tie so close and enduring, that no man on earth, by the firmest bonds of the closest friendship, by the holiest rights of the nearest kindred, could be related to me more truly, or devoted to me more intimately. From Him I may and should expect greater things than from the person in the world most devoted to me; because His love to me is to an infinite extent more fervent than the love of the most tried and steadfast friend, than the love of brother to brother, than any love on earth.

HE could rejoice like me, He could mourn and even wonder like me. Not only has He taken upon Himself the body but the soul of man, so that it was in real earnest He marvelled at the centurion's faith.

There is no article of our Faith that sustains us in all trial like this.

II.

SICKNESS.

Christ suffering in Christians.

TO THE ELECTOR FREDERIC OF SAXONY IN SICKNESS.—1527.

OUR most blessed Saviour and most gracious Master has commanded us all to visit the sick, to set free those that are bound, and to fulfil all works of mercy towards our neighbors. As Christ Himself, our Lord, with the example of a wonderful love, to manifest and prove the same, came down from the bosom of the most High Father, humbled Himself into our prison, took on Himself our infirmities, served and toiled for our sins, as He says in Isaiah, "Thou hast made Me to serve with thy sins. Thou hast wearied Me with thine iniquities."

And whosoever despiseth this most dear, fair, and loving example, and this most holy command, will surely hear at the Last Day, "Depart, ye cursed, into everlasting fire. I was sick and ye visited Me not," as one perverted by the basest ingratitude, in not showing, in his little measure, to his neighbor that which with so great a perfection of mercy he received from the Lord Christ.

Therefore, I may not neglect, without the guilt of such ingratitude, this form and likeness of my Lord Christ, in your Grace's sickness. It is to me as if I heard from the body and flesh of your Grace, the voice of Christ calling to me and saying, "I am sick." For it is not the Christian man only who is sick when he is sick, but Christ our Lord and Saviour, in whom the Christian lives, as He Himself says, "In that ye did it to the least of these my brethren, ye did it unto Me."

To Justus Menius,

IN LUTHER'S OWN SICKNESS.—1520.

I PRAY thee, cease not to pray for me and to console me; for this agony is beyond my strength.

Christ has hitherto been my faithful Preserver, neither do I despair that such He will be forever. Not only have I been sick in body, but far more in spirit, so does Satan with his angels weary me, by the permission of God our Saviour. Therefore I commend myself to your prayers, certain that the Lord will hear you, and will trample Satan under our feet. Amen.

I would have written to Ickelsamer, but the weakness of my head does not permit me to occupy myself with studies; but tell him before he asks it, that I will know nothing against him; as also I will have compassion on all my other enemies, and will know nothing against them; even as I trust Christ and the righteous Father may have compassion on me, and will know nothing against me.

Zwingli and Æcolompadius have answered, but I have not read, nor can I read until I am restored; I am altogether idling and taking holiday, as a languid Lazarus and patient of Christ.

To Agricola.—1527.

SATAN has raged against me with all his fury; yea, the Lord has set me up before him like another Job, as a mark; he tempts me with a marvellous feebleness of spirit, but through the prayers of the saints I shall not be left in his hands, although the wounds of spirit which I have received can with difficulty be healed.

My hope is that this my agony is for the sake of many; my life is that I know and glory that I have taught the Word of Christ purely and sincerely for the salvation of many, and that therefore it is that Satan burns against me, and desires to see me submerged and ruined; me, with the Word.

To comfort his Father in his last Sickness.—1530.

A GREAT joy it would be to me if you would come to me with my mother. My Käthe also begs it with tears, and all of us.

God has sealed the faith in you, and confirmed it, with signs following, namely: that for my sake you have suffered much calumny, shame, scorn, mockery, hatred, and danger.

These are the true *stigmata* (the marks of the wounds), whereby we must become like our Lord Christ.

So now, in your weakness, let your heart be fresh and comforted; for we have yonder, in that life with God, a sure, true Helper, Jesus Christ, who for us has overcome sin and death, who is sitting there for us, and with all the angels is looking upon us, and is waiting for us, when we journey forth, that we may have no care nor fear lest we should sink or fall. He has too great power over sin and death than that they should do anything to harm us; and He is so heart-true and good, that He neither can nor will forsake us. Only let us, without doubting, desire this.

But if it is His divine will that you should not longer linger away from that better life, and should no further suffer with us in this troubled valley of many sorrows, nor here any more see and hear distress, nor with all Christians here help any longer to suffer and conquer. He will surely give you grace to receive all willingly and obediently.

Herewith I commend you to Him who holds you dearer than you hold yourself, and has shown you such love that He has taken your sin on Himself, and atoned for it with His blood, and has let you know this through the Gospel, and has given you to believe it through His Spirit.

Whatever happens, let Him care. He will make all right; yea, He has already done all things for the very best, better than we can comprehend.

The same our dear Lord and Saviour be with you, and grant us to see each other again joyfully here or yonder. * For our faith is sure, and we doubt not that we shall see each other again with Christ, in a little while, since the departure from this life to God is far less than if I parted from you and went from Mansfeld hither, or than if you departed from me from Wittenberg to Mansfeld. A little hour of sleep, and all is changed.

To Margaret, Princess of Anhalt, in Sickness.

SINCE now your princely Grace is visited and heavy-laden with sickness by our dear Father in heaven, who has made us, and given us soul and body, and also, through His dear

---
* See page 18.

Son Jesus Christ, has redeemed us from the fall and death of Adam, and by His Holy Spirit has planted the hope of eternal life in our hearts, your Grace must not be distressed, but receive this visitation with thankfulness. For we who believe on Him are no more our own, but His who died for us. If we are sick it is not to ourselves; if we are well, it is not to ourselves; go with us how it may, it is all not to ourselves but to Him who has died for us, and made us His own.

As with a good child, if it is sick and suffers, its sickness is more to its parents than to itself; so is it with us and Him who has redeemed us with His blood and death. And in this faith, though we die, we die not; though we are sick, we are not sick, but whole to Christ, in whom all that according to the flesh seems to us sick, feeble, dead, and lost, is sound, fresh, living, and blessed. He is Almighty on whom we believe.

"MY TIMES ARE IN THY HAND." This saying I learned in my sickness, and will correct and alter my interpretation of it; for before I put it off as belonging only to the day of death. But it means this: In Thine hand is my time, that is, my whole life, all my days, hours, and moments. As if he should say, "My health, sickness, misfortune, prosperity, life, death, joy, sorrow, all are in Thy hands, as also experience shows."

SICKNESS.

IF trial makes us impatient, then the devil laughs and is glad.

IN the year 1536, on the 18th of July, after the sermon, Dr. Martin Luther went to visit an honorable, pious matron who had been exiled from Leipzig. On the way her husband had been drowned, and she had fallen into such heart-anguish and sorrow that in one night she had fainted away fifteen times. When the Doctor entered, she received him cordially and said, "Oh, dear Herr Doctor, how can I merit such kindness from you?"

He answered and said: "It was long since merited. Christ Jesus with His blood has done and merited far more than this."

Then he asked how it was with her, and entreated that she would be content with the will of God, and suffer it with patience, as the chastening of a Father who had redeemed her. "Dear daughter," said he, "be at peace, and suffer the Father's chastening, let it be for death or life, as it pleases God whom we love. For, living or dying, we are His, as he says, '*Because I live, ye shall live also.*' He has given you a costly treasure in this suffering. He will also give you to bear it patiently. Therefore pray diligently."

Thereupon she answered in a right Christian way, that "she was indeed at peace; she knew God meant well, and as a Father with her, and would give her patience to bear the Cross."

So the Doctor departed from her, giving her his blessing, and committed her to the care and keeping of our good God.

IN the year 1536, on the 4th of August, he visited Benedicta, the widow of the Burgomaster of Wittenberg, and he said to her: "Dear friend, you will have patience, and willingly bear the will of God, which is good and holy; for the body must suffer and die. But we have this great comfort and prerogative, that we may commit the dear soul into the bosom of Him who has redeemed us. This consolation the world has not."

HE once visited a chancery-writer at Torgau, who was a good, diligent man, comforted him, and bade him be of good heart and keep to the physician's directions, and commend his soul to the faithful Creator; "for," said he, "we may well be glad to die; we have lived long enough, save that we may have to live yet a while longer for the sake of others."

ONCE when Dr. Martin lay ill himself, and the physician felt his pulse, and found him changed for the worse, he said, "Here I am. I stand and rest here on the will of God. To Him I have entirely given myself up. He will make it all right. For this I know certainly; I shall not die, for He is the Resurrection and the

Life, and whosoever liveth and believeth on Him shall never die, and even if he die he shall live. Therefore I commit it all to His will, and leave Him to order all."

DOCTOR MARTIN LUTHER was visiting an honorable matron who lay in sore sickness, and he comforted her thus:

"Muhme Lene, do you know me? Do you recognize me?" And when she signified that she knew and understood, he said to her, "Your faith rests wholly and entirely on the Lord Christ."

Then he added:

"He is the Resurrection and the Life. You will lose nothing. You will not die, but fall asleep as in a cradle. And when the morning dawns, you will rise again and live forever."

She said, "Yes."

Then the Doctor asked her, and said:

"Have you any temptation?"

She said, "No."

"How? Does nothing indeed trouble you?"

"Yes," she said, "I have a pain in my heart."

Then he said, "The Lord will soon redeem you from all evil. You will not die."

And he turned to us and said:

"Oh, how well it is with her! For this is not death. It is sleep."

And he went to the window and prayed.

At mid-day he left her; and at seven in the evening she softly fell asleep in Christ.

Luther's Way of visiting the Sick.

WHEN Dr. Martin Luther came to visit a sick person in his weakness, he was wont to speak very gently to him; to bend down close to him, and first to ask him about his sickness, what ailed him, how long he had been ill, what physician he had seen, and what treatment had been prescribed for him.

Then he began to ask if he had been patient toward God under this sickness. And if he found that the sick person had borne his sickness patiently, as sent to him by the gracious and fatherly will of God, that he felt he deserved this chastening for his sins, and was willing, if it was the will of God, to die, then Dr. Luther began heartily to commend this Christian will and disposition as the work of the Holy Spirit. And he was wont to say it was a great gift of God when any one attained in this life the true knowledge of God and faith in Jesus Christ our only Saviour, and could yield up his will to the will of God; and he would exhort the sick person to keep steadfast in this faith, through the help of the Holy Spirit, and would promise himself to pray earnestly for him to God.

If the sufferer thanked him for this kindness, and said he did not deserve that he should visit him, the Doctor would say, "It was his office and duty, and it was needless to thank him;" and then would comfort him, saying he should be of good cheer, and fear nothing, for God was his gracious God and Father, and had given letters and seals to assure us, through His Word and Sacraments, that we poor sinners are redeemed from the devil and hell, because the Son of God willingly gave Himself up to death for us, and has reconciled us to God.

III.

BEREAVEMENT.

To Maria Queen of Hungary on the Death of her Husband, Louis II., King of Hungary,
[Who was defeated and slain in battle against the Turks, A.D. 1526.]

WITH FOUR PSALMS OF CONSOLATION.

ST. PAUL writes to the Romans that the Holy Scriptures are Scriptures of consolation, and teach us patience. Wherefore I have now sent forth these same Psalms to comfort your Majesty (as far as God comforts us, and enables us to comfort others). In this great and sudden misfortune and anguish wherewith the Almighty God at this time visits your Majesty, not in anger or displeasure, but to chasten and to try; that your Majesty may learn to trust alone in the true Father who is in heaven; and to comfort yourself in the true Bridegroom Jesus Christ, who is also Brother to each one of us, yea, our flesh and blood; and to rejoice in those true friends and faithful companions the dear angels, who are around us, and who are ministering to us.

For although it is indeed a heavy, bitter death to your Majesty, and must indeed be so, so early widowed and despoiled of your dear consort, yet will the Scriptures, especially the Psalms, give you much good comfort, richly manifesting to you the sweet, gracious Father and Son in whom the sure and eternal life lies hidden.

And, indeed, whosoever can attain to see and feel the Father's love to us in the Scriptures, he can easily bear all the unhappiness that can be on earth. On the contrary, he who feels not thus, can never be truly glad, though he were bathed in all the delights and joys of the world.

Verily, to no man can such sorrow come, as to God the Father Himself, when His beloved Son, in return for all His miracles and mercies, was wounded, spit upon, cursed, and made to die the most shameful of all deaths upon the Cross; although to each of us his own misery seems the greatest, and goes more to the heart than the Cross of Christ.

On the Death of the Wife of Capellanus.

CHRIST did not hear our prayers and tears for her preservation; but at the last He comforted us, when, with the best end, that is, full of faith and strong in spirit, she emigrated to Christ.

To Conrad Cordatus, on the Loss of a Son.

GRACE and peace in Christ, who will console thee in this thy low estate and sorrow, my Cordatus; for who else can assuage such a grief? Easily, indeed, do I believe all that thou writest, knowing how such a loss goes into the heart of a father, sharper than any sword, piercing even to the dividing asunder of the joints and marrow.

Yet, on the other hand, thou shouldst remember it is nothing marvellous if He who is more truly and essentially the Father than thou wert, in His love, chose rather to have thy son, who is verily His son, with Himself than with thee. For he is safer there than here.

But this I write in vain. As a fable to the deaf are words to recent grief; wherefore, now, yield to thy grief; for greater and better than we have mourned with such a mourning, nor were they reproved.

It is good, nevertheless, for thee to have reached once that wilderness of temptation, and to have learned the force of thine own feelings, that thou mayest learn the better in thyself what is the strength of the Word of faith.

Greet her who is the sharer of thy grief, and meanwhile rejoice more in Christ living, than ye mourn over your son dead. Yea, himself also living, though withdrawn from you.

To Melanchthon
ON THE DEATH OF LUTHER'S FATHER.—A. D. 1530.

TO-DAY Hans Reinicke has written me that my most dear father departed from this life, on the Sunday *exaudi*, at one o'clock.

This death has thrown me altogether into mourning; remembering not only the natural tie, but his most gentle tenderness to me, for from him my Creator gave me whatsoever I am and have. Although it comforts me that he writes me he fell asleep most sweetly in the faith of Christ, yet the memory of his most sweet converse has been such a shock to my heart, that scarcely ever before did I so contemn death. But "the righteous is taken away from the evil to come, and enters into rest."

So many times, indeed, do we die before we die once. I now succeed to the inheritance of the name, for I am the eldest Luther in my family. To me, now, is due not only the chance, but the right to follow him into the Kingdom of Christ, which may He benignantly grant to us all.

Therefore further I will not write to thee, for it is meet and dutiful that I, a son, should mourn for such a father, from whom the Father of mercy formed me, and through the sweat of whose brow He trained and fed me to be such as I am.

I rejoice that he lived in these times, so that he might see the light of Truth.

Blessed be God in all His acts and counsels forever. Amen.

To N. Link,

TO COMFORT HIM FOR THE LOSS OF HIS SON WHILE STUDYING AT WITTENBERG, A.D. 1532.

GRACE and peace in Christ our Lord. My dear Friend—I think the tidings must by this time have reached you that your dear son Johannes Link, who was sent hither to us to study, was seized with heavy sickness, and although, indeed, no kind of pains and care and medical skill have been spared for him, nevertheless the sickness proved too strong for him, and has borne him hence, and brought him to our Lord Jesus Christ in heaven.

He was a dear boy to us all, especially to me; for many an evening have I had him to sing the Descant in my house. Very quiet and gentle he was, and especially diligent in study, so that it is sore to all our hearts that he is gone, and if it had been possible by any means, we would fain have rescued and retained him. But he was much dearer to God than to us, and He willed to have him at home.

I know well how this event must distress and grieve your heart and your wife's, when it has so distressed us all, and especially me. Yet I entreat you rather to thank God, who has given you such a good child, and has held you worthy to spend your means and pains so well on him.

But this, most of all, must comfort you (as it comforts us), that he fell asleep so softly and serenely (fell asleep rather than departed), with such a high confession, with such faith and consciousness, as were a wonder to us all; so that there can be as little doubt as that the Christian religion can be false, that he is now forever blessed with God, his true Father. For such a Christian end cannot fail of the kingdom of heaven.

You will also take to heart how much there is to make you thankful, and to comfort you in his not having died in a painful and violent way. And if he had lived a long life, with all your pains and cost, you could only have helped him a little to some office or ministry. But now he is in that place which he would not willingly exchange for the whole world, not even for a moment.

Therefore let your grief be such that your consolation shall be more; for ye have not lost him, but sent him before you, that he may be kept forever blessed. For thus saith St. Paul: "Sorrow not as others who have no hope." I know that Master Veit Dietrich, his preceptor, will write for you some of the beautiful words which he spoke before his end, which will please and comfort you. But from love to the dear boy I would not delay to send you this letter, that you may have sure testimony how it went with him.

To Christ, our Lord and Comforter, in His grace, I commend you.

ST. GEORGE'S EVE, 1532.

D. M. L., with my own hand, though now weak.

To Laurentius Joch, Chancellor at Magdeburg,

ON THE LOSS OF HIS WIFE.

VERILY, the Son of God had to suffer, not only from the devil and the evil world, but at last men said that He was afflicted by God. So must it be with us Christians, so that it may seem to the world that God chastens us, and that our enemies may boast and say, "That is the way your new Gospel is rewarded."

It is indeed a great consolation that your wife departed in so Christian a way, and has gone without doubt to Christ her Lord, whom she learned to know here below. But it is also a great consolation that Christ has given you to be moulded into His likeness, to suffer not only from the devil, but also from God, who is and shall be your Comforter.

Therefore, although the flesh complains and cries, as Christ Himself cried on God, and was weak, yet shall the spirit be ready and willing, and exclaim with unutterable sighing, "Abba, Father!" that is, "Sharp is Thy rod, but Father art Thou still. This I know for a certainty."

Our dear Lord and Saviour, who is also our dear Example and Pattern in all our suffering, comfort you, and imprint Himself on your heart, so that you may accomplish this sacrifice, from your smitten heart, and offer up your Isaac to Him.

SUNDAY AFTER ALL-SAINTS, 1532.

To Laurentius Joch.
A SECOND LETTER OF CONSOLATION.

I HAVE read and perceived with joy that God has comforted your heart, even through the fellow-working of my letter. May the same gracious Father perfect the consolation He has begun. For we Christians must use ourselves to seek patience and comfort of the Scriptures.

It is therefore that He often withdraws from us the *consolationes rerum* that the *consolationes Scripturarum* may find space to work in us, and may no longer keep standing vainly outside, as a mere alphabet without exercise.

We must turn our faces to the *invisibilia gratiæ*, and the *non apparentia solatii*. We must turn our backs on the visible things, that we may grow used to leave them and to depart from them.

But the unwonted ever gives us pain, and the old Adam draws us back again to the visible. There would we fain rest and stay, but it cannot be. For " the things which are seen are temporal."

But both patience and consolation are God's works, impossible to our strength. This is the school of all Christians. This art they have to learn daily, and yet can they never apprehend it, much less learn it thoroughly, but remain always children, and say over and over again our A B C in this art.

For the rest, where we fail, we must cling to the forgiveness of sins, and offer our sacrifice through Christ, with a Pater Noster, until that happy Day comes, and makes us perfect in all things. Then we shall be a goodly company, in all things like Christ our Pattern.

Magdalene Luther's Illness and Death.

ON the 5th of September, 1542, Magdalene became ill, and Doctor Luther wrote to Marcus Crodel:

Grace and peace, my Marcus Crodel: I request that you will conceal from my son John what I am writing to you. My daughter Magdalene is literally almost at the point of death; soon about to depart to her Father in heaven, unless it should yet seem fit to God to spare her. But she herself so sighs to see her brother, that I am constrained to send a carriage to fetch him. They loved each other indeed dearly. May she survive to his coming; I do what I can, lest afterward the sense of having neglected anything should torture me. Desire him, therefore, without mentioning the reason, to return hither at once, with all speed in this carriage, hither where she will either be sleeping in the Lord, or will be restored. Farewell in the Lord.

[Her brother came, but she was not restored.]

As she lay very ill, Doctor Martin said:

"She is very dear to me; but, gracious God, if it is Thy will to take her hence, I am content to know that she will be with Thee."

And as she lay in the bed, he said to her:

"Magdalenchen, my little daughter, thou wouldst gladly stay with thy father here; and thou wilt also gladly go to thy Father yonder."

She said, "Yes, dearest father; as God wills."

Then the father said:

"Thou darling child, the spirit is willing, but the flesh is weak."

Then he turned away and said:

"She is indeed very dear to me; if the flesh is so strong, what will the spirit be?"

And among other things he said:

"For a thousand years God has given no bishop such great gifts as He has given me; for we must rejoice in God's gifts. I am angry with myself that I cannot rejoice from my heart for her and give thanks; although now and then I can sing a little song to our Lord God, and thank Him a little for this.

"But let us take courage. Living or dying we are the Lord's. *Sive vivimus, sive morimur,*

Domini sumus; that is both in the genitive, 'the Lord's,' and in the nominative, lords." (To Master Rörer) : "Herr Magister, be of good cheer."

Then Master George Rörer said:

"I once heard a word from your reverence, which often comforts me, namely : 'I have prayed our Lord God that He will give me a blessed dying hour, when I journey hence ; and He will also do it ; of that I feel sure. At my last hour I shall speak with Christ, my Lord, were it for ever so brief a time.' But I (said Master Rörer) have a fear that I shall depart hence suddenly, in silence, without being able to speak a word."

Then Doctor Martin Luther said :

"Living or dying we are the Lord's. Equally so, whether you fell from the top of a stair, or were suddenly to die while you were sitting quietly writing. It would not really harm me if I fell from a ladder and lay at its foot dead, for the devil is our enemy."

When at last little Magdalene's countenance changed, and she lay at the point of death, her father fell on his knees by her bedside, wept bitterly, and prayed that God would set her free.

Then she departed, and fell asleep in her father's hands.

Her mother was also in the room, but further off, on account of her grief.

This happened a little after nine o'clock on the Wednesday of the Seventeenth Sunday after Trinity, Anno 1542.

The Doctor repeatedly said, as mentioned above, "I would fain keep my child, for she is very dear to me, if our Lord God would leave her with me. But His will be done. To her indeed nothing better can happen."

While she yet lived, he said to her:

"Dear daughter, thou hast also a Father in heaven. Thou art going to him."

Then Doctor Philip said:

"The love of parents is an image and type of the Godhead, engraven in the human heart. If then, as the Scriptures say, there is in God such great love to the human race, great as that of parents to their children, verily it is a great and fervent love."

When she was now laid in the coffin, Dr. Martin Luther said:

"Thou dear Lenichen, how well it is with thee."

And as he gazed on her lying there, he said:

"Ah, thou dear Lenichen, thou shalt rise again, and shine like a star, yes, like the sun."

They had made the coffin too narrow and short for her, and he said:

"The bed is too small for her, now that she has died. I am indeed joyful in spirit, but, after the flesh, I am very sad; the flesh cannot bear it. Parting grieves one sorely, beyond measure. Wonderful it is to know that she is certainly at peace, and that all is well with her, and yet to be so sorrowful."

And when the people who came to lay out the corpse, according to custom, spoke to the Doctor and said they were grieved for his affliction, he said:

"You should be pleased. I have sent a saint to heaven; yes, a living saint! Oh that we might have such a death. Such a death I would welcome this very hour."

Then some one said: "Yes, that is indeed true; yet each would fain keep his own."

Doctor Martin answered:

"Flesh is flesh, and blood is blood. I am glad that she has passed over. There is no sorrow but that of the flesh."

Afterward he said to others who came in:

"Let it not grieve you. I have sent a saint to heaven. Yes, I have sent two thither."*

As they were chanting by the corpse, " Lord, remember not against us our former sins which are of old;" he said, "I say, O Lord, Lord, not only our former sins which are of old, but our present and actual sins, for we are usurers, exactors, misers. Yea, the abomination of the mass is still in the world."

---

* Alluding to the death of his infant child, Elizabeth, of whom he wrote in 1528 to Hausmann:

"My little daughter is dead; my darling little Elizabeth. It is strange how sick and wounded she has left my heart, almost as tender as a woman's, such pity moves me for that little one. I never could have believed before what is the tenderness of a father's heart for his children. Do thou pray to the Lord for me, in whom, farewell."

When the coffin was closed and she was laid in the grave, he said:

"There is indeed the Resurrection of the body."

And as they returned from the funeral, he said:

"My daughter is now provided for, both in body and soul. We Christians have nothing to complain of; we know it must be so. We are more sure of eternal life than of anything else. For God who has promised it to us for His dear Son's sake can never lie. Two saints of my flesh our Lord God has taken, but not of my blood. Flesh and blood cannot inherit the Kingdom."

Among other things he said:

"We must, however, provide for our children, and especially for the poor little maidens. We must not leave it to others to care for them. For the boys I have no mercy. A lad can maintain himself wherever he goes if he will only work; and if he will not work he is a scoundrel. But the poor little maiden-folk must have a staff in their hands.

And again:

"I give this daughter very willingly to God. Yet after the flesh, I would have wished to keep her longer with me. But since He has taken her away I thank Him."

The night before Magdalene died, her mother had a dream in which it seemed to her that two fair youths, gloriously apparelled, came and sought to lead her daughter away to her marriage.

When on the next morning Philip Melanchthon came into the cloister (Luther's home), and asked her how her daughter was, she told him her dream.

But he was alarmed at it, and said to others:

"Those young men are the dear angels who will come and lead this maiden into the kingdom of heaven, to the true marriage.

And on the same day indeed she died.

Some little time after her death Dr. Martin Luther said:

"If my daughter Magdalene would come to life again, and bring with her to me the Turkish kingdom, I would not have it so. Ah, she has made a good journey. *Beati mortui qui in Domino moriuntur.* Who dies thus, surely has eternal life. I would that I and my children and ye all, my friends, could thus journey hence, for evil days are coming. There is neither help nor counsel more on earth, until the Last Day. I hope, if God will, it will not be long delayed; for covetousness and usury increase."

And often at supper he repeated, "*Et multiplicata sunt mala in terris.*"

Luther's Epitaph on Magdalene.

DORMIO cum sanctis hic Magdalena Lutheri
 Filia, et hoc strato tecta quiesco meo.
Filia mortis eram, peccati semine nata,
 Sanguine sed vivo, Christe, redempta tuo.

BEREAVEMENT.

(IN ENGLISH.)

HERE sleep I, Lenichen, Dr. Luther's little daughter,
Rest with all the Saints in my little bed:
I who was born in sins,
And must forever have been lost.
But now I live, and all is well with me,
Lord Christ, redeemed with Thy blood.

To Justus Jonas.

I THINK you will have heard that my most dear daughter Magdalene is born again to the eternal Kingdom of Christ. But although I and my wife ought to do nothing but give thanks, rejoicing in so happy and blessed a departure, by which she has escaped the power of the flesh, the world, the Turk, and the devil; yet such is the strength of natural affection that we cannot part without groans and sobs of heart. They cleave to our heart; they remain fixed in its depths; her face, her words, the looks, living and dying, of that most dutiful and obedient child; so that even the death of Christ (and what are all deaths in comparison with that?) scarcely can efface her death from our minds. Do thou, therefore, give thanks to God in our stead. Wonder at the great work of God who thus glorifies our flesh! She was, as thou knowest, gentle and sweet in disposition, and was altogether lovely. Blessed be the Lord Jesus Christ who called, and chose, and has thus magnified her! I wish for myself and all mine, that we may attain to such a death; yea, rather to such a life, which only I ask from God, the Father of all consolation and mercy.

To Jacob Probst, Pastor at Bremen.

MY most dear daughter Magdalene has departed to her Father in heaven. I have overcome that paternal passion of my grief; but not without quivering with vengeance against death, with which indignant passion I have assuaged my tears. I loved her vehemently. But in that Day we shall be avenged on death, and on him who is the author of death.

My Kätha salutes thee, still sobbing, and with eyes wet with weeping.

To Amsdorf.

I THANK thee that thou hast sought to console me on the death of my most dear daughter. I loved her with a right and perfect love, not only because she was my flesh, but for her most placid and gentle spirit, ever so dutiful to me. But now I rejoice that she lives with her Father, in most sweet sleep, until that Day. And such as our times are, and worse as they will continue to become, I from my inmost heart desire for myself and for all men, for thee also and all dear to us, that a like hour of transition may be given to us, with so great faith, and such placid quiet to fall asleep in the Lord; not to see death, nor to taste it, nor in the least degree to feel its terrors. I hope the time is now at hand of that word of Isaiah's: "The just are gathered and lie down on their beds in peace," that when He gathereth the wheat into His garner, He may deliver the chaff to His fire.

Kätha salutes thee, still sobbing from time to time at the recollection of that most obedient child.

To Lauterbach.

THOU writest well, that in this most evil age death is indeed to be desired (or rather sleep), for our daughters, and for all dear to us. And yet this departure of my most dear child has moved me not a little. Nevertheless I rejoice, sure that she, as a child of the Kingdom, has been snatched from the jaws of the devil and of the world, so sweetly did she fall asleep in the faith of Christ.

To Justus Jonas

ON THE DEATH OF HIS WIFE.—1542

WHAT to write I scarcely know, so has this sudden grief of thine prostrated me.

A most sweet sharer of life have we all lost. She was not only, in truth, dear to me, but her most pleasant face, always full of consolation, was dear to us all, for we knew that in all which concerned us of good or ill, she did not only feel with us, but made it all her own to share and to bear. Bitter is this parting, when I had hoped she would be left after me, to be to all mine the first and chief comforter among all women.

I am stunned by this great sorrow, when I remember her most gentle character, her most placid manner, her most faithful heart. I cannot restrain my sobs at the loss of such a woman, so surpassing in piety and honor, in modesty and all human kindness. What it must be to thee, from my own example I can easily measure. The flesh has no comfort for such a grief. We must take refuge with the spirit, for with a happy ending of her course, she has gone before to Him who has called us all, and will bring us all through, to Himself, in His own blessed hour, from this misery and malice of the world. Amen.

Meanwhile do thou, I entreat, so sorrow (for cause indeed there is), that thou keep in mind the common lot of us Christians, who although according to the flesh we are separated with most grievous rendings asunder, yet in that life shall see each other again, gathered and knit together in all those sweet unions of old, in Him who has so loved us that He has obtained that life for us with His own blood and death. *Dying and behold we live*, as saith Paul.

It is well done for us, when with a pure faith in the Son of God we fall asleep. True indeed that thy greatest pity should be for those who live. We here, for a little while in sorrow, shall be received out of it into that unutterable joy, to which thy Kätha and my Magdalene, with many others, have gone before us, and to which every day they call, exhort, and tenderly allure us that we may follow.

To Wolf Heinze
ON THE DEATH OF HIS WIFE.

THIS very hour Dr. Jonas has told me that your dear Eva has gone home to God her Father. I can indeed feel how such a parting must go to your heart, and your heart-sorrow is indeed a grief of heart to me; for you know that I have a deep and faithful love for you. I know also that God has love for you; for His Son Jesus is dear to you. Therefore your grief moves me much.

Now what shall we do? This life is thus based on sorrow that we may learn how little all misery is compared with the eternal misery from which the Son of God has redeemed us, He in whom we have our dearest Treasure, which abides with us forever, though all that is temporal, and we ourselves, must pass away.

It is better with her now than where she was. God help you and all of us to journey thence after her, although without sorrow that journey, will not, cannot be made.

To Hans Reineck
ON THE DEATH OF HIS WIFE.

DEEP sorrow indeed must this be to you. My heart also is very heavy for your sake.

But what can we do? God has so ordered and balanced this life, that therein we have to learn and practise the knowledge of His Divine and perfect will, so that we may prove ourselves whether we love and esteem His will more than our own selves, and than all He has given us to love and possess on earth.

And although the infinite goodness of His Divine will is hidden too high and deep, as is God Himself, from the old Adam, so that He can draw no delight or joy, but only mourning and wailing from it, yet we have His holy, sure Word, which reveals to us that hidden will, and makes it shine in our hearts; as everywhere in the Scriptures He says to us, it is not in anger, but in grace, when He chastens His children.

Therefore, since you have richly learned the Word of God, I hope you will know how to practise it, that you have the more joy in God's grace and Fatherly will, and that the sorrow may not be to your hurt.

It is, moreover, a high consolation that your wife departed in such a Christian way from this valley of sorrow.

The dearest treasure on earth is a dear wife; but a blessed end is a treasure beyond all treasures, and an eternal consolation.

God help us all in a like way to journey from this sinful sepulchre of corruption to our true Home and Fatherland.

To George Hosel
ON THE LOSS OF A SON.—A.D. 1544.

OUR Saviour Christ saith, "*It is not the will of your heavenly Father that one of these little ones should perish.*" He adds also a sign, namely, that "*Their angels do always see the Face of God.*" Therefore you must not doubt that your child is with our Saviour Christ and all the Blessed in joy.

I also am a father, and have seen some of my children die. I have also seen other miseries greater than death, and I know that such things cause anguish. God wills that our children should be dear to us. He wills that we should weep for them. Yet the faith of the eternal joy must work consolation in us.

To Ambrosius Berndt
ON THE DEATH OF HIS WIFE.

"THIS calamity is indeed a burning fire to thee, yet is there sweetness distilling from the very anguish. For it is well with her. She lives now with Christ. She has sprung forth (taken her spring into the other life.)" Ah, would to God that I also had taken that spring. I would not much wish myself here again.

(Sie hat ihren Sprung gethan. O, wollt Gott dass ich den Sprung auch gethan hätte. Ich wollt mich nicht sehr herwieder sehnen.)

ON the 1st of December, 1536, Dr. Martin Luther visited the Burgomaster Lucas Cranach (the painter), who was very sorrowful and distressed on account of the death of his dear and dutiful son, who by the advice and wish of his parents, and other good people, had travelled to Italy, and at Bologne, on the evening of the 9th of October, had died, with a beautiful, glorious Christian confession of faith.

But his parents, besides their natural love and tenderness, distressed and tortured themselves as if they had been the cause of his death, because they had sent him thither.

Thereupon said Dr. Martin: "If this were so, I am certainly as much a cause of this as you, for I faithfully counselled you and him to it. But we did not do it with the intention that he should die. Our hearts bear witness with us how far rather we would have had him living. Yea, you would indeed far rather have died yourselves, or lost everything you possess."

Afterwards he turned to the father, who was weeping, and said: "Dear Master Lucas, let your heart be quieted. God wills to break your will, for He smites us where the pain is sorest, to crucify the old Adam. And even if our trials are not the greatest, to us they seem so.

"Think of dear Adam, what heart-anguish his was when the first-born brother murdered the second.

"Think of the beloved David, who mourned

for Amnon and for Absalom, and Absalom was indeed lost.

"Let us be comforted by the thought of your son's goodness and dutifulness. For the world is so evil that the choicest youths come to shame, and your son might even have experienced this.

"Grievous it is to you to have lost a good, obedient son. We cannot but remember the good and true more than the evil and disobedient; yet let his obedience and his Christian departure be a joy to you. For his last hour was indeed good and blessed, and God chose when it should be. Ah, blessed, and twice blessed is he who has such a departure. It is my daily sigh and prayer that God may grant me a blessed, joyful departure. Then shall I see that all was well with me here, and, redeemed from all distress and sorrow, be joyful with God.

"Dear Master Lucas, commit this to God. He is the highest Father, and has more right to your son than even you have. For you are only his earthly father—have only trained and cherished him a little while. But God has given him body and soul, has guarded and kept him until now; is a tenderer, yes, a far tenderer Father than you. He knows how, and He will preserve him, care for him, cherish him better than even you, on the whole, could do. Let your mourning and grief have measure; commit it to the will of God, which is better than ours. Eat and drink and refresh yourself; do not make yourself ill with grief, for you shall yet serve and help many."

To Justus Jonas
ON THE DEATH OF HEINZ'S WIFE.—1543.

I KNOW his sorrow and mourn with him. But the time is coming in which thanks will be given to God, who has taken away His own, by so fatherly a stroke, and one suited to His Church, from the abysses and Tartaruses of this world. I can now rejoice that my most dear daughter Magdalene has been called out of this Ur of the Chaldees, feeling secure for her who now abides secure in eternal peace, although with great anguish I lost her.

To Baumgärtner's Wife
ON THE PERILOUS IMPRISONMENT OF HER HUSBAND.—1544.

OUR griefs have not risen so high nor grown so bitter as those of His dear Son and the dear mother of His Son.

We have this glorious great advantage in our sorrows over the sorrow of the world, that God is gracious and favorable unto us, with all His angels and creatures, so that no misfortune to the body can hurt the soul, but must rather be for our profit.

You suffer not alone, but have many, many faithful pious hearts who have great sympathy with you. Yea, truly, in great troops we visit dear Baumgärtner in his prison; that is, we visit the Lord Christ captive in this His faithful member, and pray and call on Him that He will deliver him, so that He may rejoin you and all of us.

To Parents unknown on the Death of their Son.

SO also ye, when ye have mourned and wept as ye needs must, will once more comfort yourselves; yea, thank God with joy, that your son has had so beautiful an end, and has so gently fallen asleep in Christ, that there can be no doubt he must be in the eternal rest of Christ, sleeping sweetly and softly.

For every one wondered at the great grace which enabled him to continue steadfast to the end in prayer, and in the confession of Christ, which grace must be dearer to you than that he should have revelled a thousand years in all the wealth and honors of the world. He has taken with him the greatest treasure we can gain in this life.

He has baffled the world and the devil; but we must daily be baffled by them, and wander in the midst of perils, while he is safe.

You have sent him to the best school; and your love and cost are well repaid. God help us to follow.

The Lord and highest Comforter Jesus Christ,

to whom your son is dearer than even to you; who first met him with His Word, and then demanded him Himself, and took him from you, may He comfort and strengthen you by His grace, until the day when you shall see your son again in His eternal joy.

To the Widow of George Schulze on the Death of her Husband.

THE SACRIFICE OF THE WILL TO GOD.

YET, although you must indeed have sorrow, the will of God is best of all. He has given His Son for us. How meet then is it that we should offer up our wills to His will and to His service and good pleasure, which not only are we bound to do, but therein shall we have great and eternal fruit and joy.

Part Fifth.

WORDS OF VICTORY.

WORDS OF VICTORY.

I.

THE LAST CONFLICT.

To the People of Wittenberg, A.D. 1521.

I CANNOT always be with you. Every one of us must die alone; and in that greatest and last conflict none of us can counsel or help another. I shall not be with you, nor you with me. He who stands steadfast then against sin, the devil, and hell, is saved. He who endures not is lost.

But in that hour none will stand steadfast save those who have well learned the words of power and comfort against sin during life. What the soul has embraced of that comfort in the world, that she bears away with her. That, and nothing in the world besides.

Against the devil and hell no one in that hour can stand, save he who has learned Christ by heart thoroughly; so that he can defiantly, nothing doubting, hold up against the devil how Christ died for him, and has vanquished Satan and hell. Then will he be saved, though all the devils are against him.

The Fear of Death.

"THE fear of death," he said, "is itself death, and nothing else. He who has banished death from his heart tastes and feels no death."

He was asked about the pains of death.

"Ask my Käthe," he said, "if she felt anything of them, for she was indeed dead."

She replied, "Herr Doctor, I felt nothing."

Then Doctor Martin said, "Therefore I say that the fear of death is the greatest part of death. In the Hebrews it is written that '*He* (the Lord Christ) *tasted death for every man.*' We are happy people not to have to taste death. For the taste of death is bitter! What kind of anguish it is to taste death may be seen indeed in Christ Himself, when He says, '*My soul is exceeding sorrowful even unto death.*' In the garden it was that Christ died. For to taste death is to die."

What do you think these words mean, "*My soul is exceeding sorrowful even unto death?*" I hold them to be the greatest words in the whole Scriptures, although these also are indeed great, when He cried on the Cross, "*My God, my God! why hast Thou forsaken me?*" No one can compress this into words. No angel understands how great that agony was that pressed the bloody sweat from Him.

That was the taste and terror of death, when a creature had to strengthen the Creator! The Apostles understood nothing at all of it.

"*He who keeps my Saying shall never taste Death.*"

FOR when he dies, life shall so lift itself up before him, that for this life which he sees he shall not be able to see death.

For the night becomes clear light, and bright as day, because the light and the shining of that rising, dawning, new life, altogether quenches and shines away this dying and self-destroying death.

DEATH, which is to men a penalty of sin, through the most tender and kind mercy of God becomes to Christian men an end of sin, and a beginning of life and righteousness.

For to him who already has righteousness and life, death becomes a minister of life—a loom wherein life is woven; which surely we need not fear, since through no other passage can we reach that life.

This is the might of faith. It mediates between death and life, transmuting death into life and immortality.

THEY threaten us with death.

If they were as wise as they are unwise, they would threaten us with life.

It is a contemptible, feeble threat to threaten Christ and His Christians with death, when they are lords and victors already over death.

It is as if I were to threaten a man that I would bridle his horse for him, and set him to ride thereon.

But they believe not that Christ is risen from the dead, and is Lord over life and death. To them He is still in the grave; yea, still in hell.

But we know (and knowing this are bold and joyful), that He has risen, and that death is nothing more than the end of sin and of itself.

Small Intimations of Immortality.

HEREIN is indicated the soul's immortality, in that no creature save only man can understand and measure the heavenly bodies. Animals do not consider and analyze the water they drink. This upward contemplation of his indicates that man was not made to live always in this lower part of the world, but that hereafter he should possess the heavens.

DEATH, in men, is in infinite and countless ways more mournful than in animals without reason. For man is a creature that was not created for this, but to live in obedience to the Divine Word, and in the likeness of God. Man was not created to die.

"DEAR brothers," said Dr. Martin Luther, "despise the devil. For He who was nailed to the cross has crucified him; so likewise if he crucifies us, we, on the other hand, shall crucify him, even with that cross wherewith he crucifies us."

THANK God, the devil has never been able altogether to vanquish me; he has burnt himself out on Christ. He says, "Be of good cheer, I have overcome the world; the sting of death has been worn out and blunted on Me, yea, altogether broken."

IN the year 1538, on the 21st of October, Dr. Martin Luther made a public exhortation in the church, severely blaming those who were so fearful, and made such a clamor and cry about the Plague.

"We should be of good cheer in the Lord; and should trust Him," said he, "and each of us abide and walk in his own calling, and if our neighbors need our help and assistance, not desert them. We ought not to be so sore afraid of death; for we have the Word of life, and we cleave to the Lord of life, who for our sake has overcome death."

Since now He has been laid beneath this earth, and has been buried, henceforth the graves of all Christians become sanctuaries, and wherever a Christian rests, there rests the sacred body of a Saint.

The Damsel is not dead, but sleepeth.

This place is very remarkable, that our Lord Himself calls death nothing else than sleep, which is a glorious consolation for all who believe. For Christ does not only say that the dead maiden sleeps; He proves by facts that she sleeps, in that He speaks to her with soft, gentle words, as to awaken her from sleep.

This wisdom none of the world's wise men have reached; endless questions they have raised, but here all the questions are answered in one word, "*She sleeps.*"

If she sleeps, where art thou, O Death?

Death is no death to the Christian, but really a sleep. Yes, even the place where Christians are buried is called κοιμητηριον, that is, a sleeping-chamber.

A man who lies asleep is much like one who is dead. Therefore the ancient sages said, "Sleep is the brother of Death."

So also Death and Life are pictured and signified in the revolutions and transformations of day and night, and of all creatures.

SLEEP is verily a death, and, equally, death is a sleep. Our death is nothing but a night's sleep.

In sleep all weariness passes away, and we rise again in the morning joyous, fresh, and strong.

So at the last Day shall we arise from our graves as if we had only slept a night, be fresh and strong, bathe our eyes (as in morning dew), and all weakness, corruption, and dishonor shall vanish from us forever.

IF Cicero could nobly console himself and take courage against death, how much more should we Christians, who have a Lord who is the Destroyer of death, who has vanquished him, namely, Christ the Son of God, who is the Resurrection and the Life.

AND if we would fain live a little longer, what a little while it is at the longest! Just as if several of us were journeying over the Düben Heath to Leipzig, and some arrived at four o'clock, some at seven or eight, some at evening; yet all had to be there before night. Thus our first forefather arrived a few hours before us. But even he will have rested no longer than one night, like ourselves.

WE must submit to death; but the miracle is that whosoever keeps to God's Word shall not feel death, but pass hence as one falling asleep. No more should it be said of such an one, *Morior, sed cogor dormire;* no more " I die," but, " I am constrained to sleep."

" I KNOW I shall not live long," he said ; " my brain is like a knife in which the steel is quite worn out, and there is nothing but iron left. The iron can cut no more. So it is with my brain. Now, Oh my dear Lord! I hope, and am persuaded, that the hour of my departure is at hand.

" At Cobourg I used to go about and seek a place where they might bury me ; and I thought I could rest well in the Chapel, beneath the Cross. But now I am weaker than I was at Cobourg. God help me, and give me a gracious, blessed departure. I desire not to live any longer."

ON the 22d of July, in the year 1533, Dr. Martin Luther said, at table, to Duke John Frederic, Elector of Saxony, " It is a far more terrible thing when a prince dies than when a peasant dies, who is thought nothing of.

" A prince has to be abandoned of all his friends and nobles, and at last must enter into single combat with the devil. Then there will be no help in remembering that one has lived in a princely style."

DEATH for the sake of Christ's name and Word is held precious and glorious before

God; for we are mortal, and must die in one way or another, on account of sin. But if we can die for the sake of Christ's Word, and the free confession of it, we die a most honorable death; we become altogether sacred; we have sold our life dear enough.

We who are Christians pray for peace and a long life; not for our own sakes, for to such death is pure gain; but for the sake of the Church and those who come after us.

To all the dear Friends of Christ at Halle.
—1527.

(ON THE MURDER OF THE PREACHER GEORGE WINKLER, BY ARCHBISHOP ALBRECHT, AT MAINZ.)

THEREFORE will I translate into writing the cry of his blood from the earth; that this murder may never more be silent, until God, the merciful Father and just Judge, hear this cry, as He heard that of the blood of holy Abel, and execute justice and vengeance on the murderer and traitor, the old enemy who brought about the deed; that the blood of Master George may be a Divine seed, and may bring forth fruit an hundred-fold; so that instead of one murdered George, a hundred other true-hearted preachers may arise, who shall do Satan a thousand-fold more harm than this one man has done. And thus, because he would not endure to hear this one, he shall have to endure, hear, and see countless numbers. As it happened to the Pope through the blood of Huss, whom he would not suffer to whisper in a corner, and is now constrained to suffer to cry aloud throughout all the world, until Rome itself, and the whole world are become too narrow for this cry, and nevertheless there is no end to it.

To Michael Stiefel,
ON THE MARTYRDOM OF LEONHARD KAISER.—1527.

UNHAPPY am I, so unequal to Leonhard. I a preacher of many words, he a mighty doer of the Word. Who will make me worthy, that, not with a double portion of his spirit, but with the half of it, I may vanquish Satan?

Pray for me. Christ grant that we be followers of Leonhard. Not king only is he deservedly named, but Kaiser, who has vanquished him to whose power there is no equal on the earth.

Not a priest only is he, but a high-priest and true Pope, who has thus offered his body a sacrifice to God, acceptable, living, holy. Well too he is named Leonhard; that is, strength of a lion. Truly he was a lion, strong and fearless. All names with him have been fateful. He first of his family has consecrated and fulfilled the family name.

Attestation.

"THE handwriting of Luther which he gave to a messenger who asked for a certificate that he was alive; for the Papists had shown great joy at the news of his death."

I DOCTOR MARTIN, confess, in this my handwriting, that I am of one mind with the Devil, the Pope, and all my enemies; for they would fain rejoice over my death; and I, from my heart, would fain give them this joy, and would gladly have died at Smalkald. But God would not have it so that I should confirm this their joy.

But one day He will do it ere they think, to my great gain; and then they will say, "Alas, if Luther were still alive!"

THERE is no better death than that of St. Stephen, who says, "Lord, into Thy hands I commend my spirit."* To lay aside all the register of our sins and our merits, and to die on simple grace alone.

St. Stephen learned this of two high persons, of the Lord Christ, and of David.

---

* *V.* Page 27.

II.

THE PRESENT LIFE OF THE JUST IN HEAVEN.

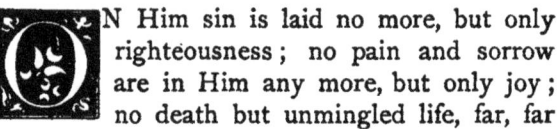

ON Him sin is laid no more, but only righteousness; no pain and sorrow are in Him any more, but only joy; no death but unmingled life, far, far fuller than this temporal life. This should make us joyful. For since the Lord Christ is now sitting yonder at the right hand of God, and possesses and rules not a kingdom of death, sorrow, and misery, but a kingdom of life, where dwell peace, joy, and redemption from all evil, so also it is certain that His own do not remain in death, anguish, terror, temptation, and suffering, but must be torn from death, and live with Him. "*Because I live, ye shall live also.*"

IT is enough that we know we live when our body dies. But how we shall there live, we know not yet. For this life is hidden in God.

"HE IS THE GOD NOT OF THE DEAD, BUT OF THE LIVING." Therefore it is impossible that the good should altogether die. They must live eternally; otherwise God would not be their God.

THE Scriptures say that the holy and just go into the unseen world, and there enjoy the most pleasant peace, and the sweetest rest. How they live there we indeed know not, nor what the place is where they dwell. But this we know assuredly, they are in no grief or pain, but rest in the grace of God. As in this life they were wont to fall softly asleep in the guard and keeping of God and of the dear angels, without fear of harm, though the devil might prowl around them, so after this life do they repose in the hand of God.

WHEN my soul journeys forth I know that highest kings and princes are appointed to attend me, namely the dear angels themselves, who will receive me and guard me on my way.

THE Father of all mercy has given us to believe not in a wooden, but in a living Christ.

And if Satan towers yet higher, and rages more fiercely, he shall not weary us out, unless he could tear down Christ from the right hand of God.

While Christ sits there, we also shall remain lords and princes over sin, death, the devil, and hell.

Our cause is not yet sunk so low as it sank in Christ's own time, when Peter himself denied Him, and all the disciples fled from Him, and Judas betrayed Him. And if it fell as low as this, nevertheless, never should it fall to the ground, nor ever shall our Christ perish.

THE world lifts itself up raging against Christ. Be it so. With this Man we choose to be trampled on, and with Him to rise. We shall see what they gain and we lose by this; for He says, "*Where I am, there also shall my servant be.*"

THE enemy will have to let Christ stand; and even if we die, we are not dead. If Christ can die, then shall I die. But I comfort myself with this. The Word of God abideth forever. "*I live, and ye shall live also.*" .

Immortality in Name and in Truth.

SINCE all men feel and recognize, yea see, that we must die and pass away, every one seeks immortality here on earth, that he may be forever remembered.

Great kings, princes, and lords sought it of old, by erecting marble obelisks, and high pyramids; and now by building costly churches and palaces. Soldiers seek an eternal name through famous victories; learned men by writing books.

But the endless, imperishable glory, and the eternity of God, men do not see. Ah! we are poor creatures.

NATURAL life is a little fragment of the Eternal life.

THIS life is life before our true birth to immortality.

ALL that God creates, He creates for life. He has delight in life.

HE said once, "When he lay a babe on his mother's breast he knew little how he would afterwards be nourished, or what his future life would be." Still less do we understand what the eternal life will be. We are like infants here.

HERE on earth it is ever imperfect. We cannot here acknowledge and grasp our true treasure as we would. He has indeed begun in us, and will not give up the work, but if we continue in faith and are not impatient, He will bring us to the true, eternal good things and perfect gifts, where we shall never wander, stumble, be angry, or sin any more.

WE know not how our Lord God is carrying on His building. Here we see only the scaffolding, with its beams and boards.

But in that life we shall see God's building and house; and then we shall wonder, and shall indeed rejoice that we have endured temptation.

AS there is a difference among the stars, so will there be among the Saints after this life, in the eternal life. As St. Augustine says, "God crowns His gifts in man."

WE do not believe that God will give us better things than those which He lavishes on the godless in this world; namely, better things than money, lands, honor, and power.

The supreme good, indeed, He withholds from them, because they desire it not; namely, Himself.

But he who has not God, let him have what he will besides, is poorer and more miserable before God than Lazarus, who lay at the rich man's gate, and died of hunger there.

If indeed the rich, patient God lavishes such temporal good things, yea, even dominions and kingdoms, on His bitter foes and blasphemers, what has He not prepared for us His children who suffer for His sake? Nay, what has He not given? His Only Begotten Son, and with Him all things: that we in Him should be children of

God, heirs and fellow-heirs, through hope, of eternal heavenly treasures.

"I HAVE been suffering from sore sickness, so that I gave up my life to God; but many a thought have I had in my weakness. Oh! how I thought of what eternal life is, what joys it has! Although I am sure that it is already given us through Christ, and prepared for us, because we believe; yet, it is there that it will be manifested what the new creation shall be. Whilst we remain here below, we cannot attain to understanding the first creation.

"If I had been with God before He created the world, I could have given Him no counsel how to create the round worlds and the firmament from nothing, and to jewel it with the Sun, enlightening all the earth in its swift course; or how to create man and woman. All this He did, and none was His counsellor or taught Him. Surely therefore I may joyfully trust Him and give Him glory for the future life, and the new creation, how all shall be in these, and be content that He alone be the Creator."

"I THINK often about it," said Dr. Martin, "but I cannot understand how we shall spend our time in that eternal life; no change, no eating and drinking, no labor, nothing to do. I deem, however, that we shall have countless objects to contemplate."

Thereon Philip Melanchthon said very softly: "*Lord, show us the Father and it sufficeth us.*" That will be the glorious object for us to contemplate. With that we shall have enough to do.

"IN the life to come," Dr. Martin said, "we shall not see darkly, as we now do; but we shall see face to face; that is to say, there shall be a most glorious brightness of the Eternal Majesty, in which we shall see God, even as He is. There shall be a true and perfect knowledge and love of God, a perfect light of reason, and a perfect will, an heavenly, Divine, and eternal will."

THIS far passeth all man's capacity, that God should call us heirs, not of some rich and mighty prince, not of the Emperor, not of the world, but of God, the Almighty Creator of all things. If a man could comprehend the great excellency of this, that he is indeed the son and the heir of God, and with a constant faith believe the same, he would contemn all the pomp and glory of the world in comparison of the eternal inheritance. He would do all things with great humility, and suffer all with great patience.

Furthermore, he would earnestly desire, with Paul, to depart and be with Christ; and nothing could be more welcome to him than speedy death, which he would embrace as a most joyful entering into peace, knowing that it would be the end of all his miseries, and that through it he should attain to his true inheritance.

Yea, a man that could perfectly believe this, would not long remain alive, but would be swallowed up at once with exceeding joy.

I BELIEVE that in that future life we shall need no occupation but to contemplate with wondering joy the Creator and His creatures.

AGAIN in his sickness, in the year 1538, he said many beautiful things about the future life, and of its "unutterable joy, which human reason cannot comprehend with all her speculation and meditation, since we cannot with our thoughts escape from the visible and corporeal. The eternal can be comprehended in no human creature's heart. Work itself will be delight there. Rapture will be work. What that joy will be we cannot conceive."

THERE we shall ever be studying, and learning more of what there is in the Incarnation of the Son of God. We can never learn that mystery through. Yes, this will be the Eternal life, the life of the angels, ever searching and learning more and more; ever seeing something new that we have not seen before.

NOT to leave us here on this earth with its troubles and sorrows, its poor wants and pleasures, did Christ come from heaven, die on the Cross, and rise again; still less to leave us in the dust and corruption of the grave; but to bring us to another life, where we shall need no more to eat and drink and toil; shall never more suffer, be sorrowful, or die.

III.

THE RESURRECTION AND THE GLORIOUS ADVENT.

Manifestation of Christ.

NOW that Christ has risen again He has drawn all with Him, so that all men must rise, even the ungodly. But that we still live here and use this world is just as if a father were to take a journey into a foreign country, and were to say to his child or servant, " See, there thou hast two golden groschen; use them for the necessities and nourishment of thy body until I come again."

Moreover all creatures are a figure and type of the future Resurrection, for towards the spring they come forth again living from death, grow and become green, which in winter no one would believe could be, who had not before proved and seen it.

Similarly, now that He has ascended to heaven He has taken all with Him thither. He sitteth on the right hand of God and has translated us who are members of His body with Him into the heavenly existence, that we also, like Christ, may be lords over all things; whilst yet He remains the First-born among many brethren.

Therefore, a Christian who believes this looks at the sun, and all that we use here in this world, as if they were not, but ever thinks of the future life, in which he already lives, although it doth not yet appear. The whole creation also waiteth for the manifestation of the sons of God.

CHRIST has made us free, not civilly and carnally, but divinely. The most high and sovereign Majesty doth not only defend and succor us in this life, but as touching our bodies also, will deliver us, so that our bodies, which are sown in corruption and dishonor and weakness, shall rise again in incorruption, glory, and power.

Death, which is the most mighty and dreadful thing in all the world, is utterly vanquished in the conscience by this liberty of the Spirit.

Wherefore the majesty of this Christian liberty is highly to be esteemed and diligently considered.

IN the year 1539, on the 11th of April, Doctor Martin Luther was in his garden, and with many a deep thought, he looked at the trees—

how fair and lovely they were, budding and blossoming and growing green; he said, "Praised be God the Creator, who in the spring-time out of dead creatures makes all living again. Look at the little twigs," he said, "so sweet and full; pregnant with new life. There we have a beautiful image of the Resurrection of the dead. The winter is death; the summer is the Resurrection of the dead, for then all live again and grow green."

OUR Lord has written the promise of the Resurrection, not in books alone, but in every leaf in spring-time.

WHILE Adam (the old man) lives; that is, while he sins, life is swallowed up of death. But when Christ dies, death is swallowed up of Life, that is, of Christ Himself.

IN the year 1544, on the Sunday *Cantate*, after Easter, Dr. Martin made a very beautiful sermon in the Church on the Resurrection of the dead, from the Epistle. He dwelt on these words: "*Thou fool, that which thou sowest is not quickened except it die.*" He spoke first of the Resurrection of Christ, "which," said he, "every day becomes more complete, as one by one we follow Him. For we must ever bind and link together the Resurrection of Christ and our own. For He is our Head."

WHEN we shall live in that Day we shall look with wonder on one another, and say, "Shame! that we were not of better cheer, braver and stronger, and more joyful to trust Christ, and to endure the Cross, and all tribulations and persecutions, since this glory is so great."

THIS corrupt and feeble body cannot continue as it is. Therefore it is best that the Potter should take the vessel, break it in pieces, make it mere clay again, and then make it altogether new.

"I SHALL rise again," said Dr. Martin, "and once more be able to converse with you. This finger, on which this ring is, I shall have again. All must be restored. For it is written, 'God will create new heavens and a new earth wherein dwelleth righteousness.' That will be no empty nor idle kingdom. There will be pure joy and rapture; for those heavens and that earth will be no dry, barren sand.

"When a man is happy, a green tree, a fair flower, or nosegay can make him glad; but when he is sad he can scarcely bear to look at the trees, or at anything beautiful.

"Heaven and earth shall be renewed, and we who believe shall be all together, one company.

"If we were all one here on earth there would be great peace; but God makes it otherwise, and suffers this world to be so strangely entangled and confused that we may long and sigh for the future Fatherland, and be weary of this toilsome life.

WHEN Christ shall cause the trumpet to peal at the last Day, then all will spring forth and arise ; as the flies who lie dead (dormant) in winter, but towards summer, when the sun shines, start to life again ; as the birds, who lie dead (dormant) all the winter in nests, or in clefts of the rocks and trees, or under the hollow banks of streams, as the cuckoo, the swallow, and others, and towards spring come to life again. Experience teaches us to expect this.

ONCE, when Dr. Martin and others had been discoursing merrily together, they came at length to earnest converse about eternal life; "how the heavens and the earth would be made new." In Christ we already possess the new future and eternal life. Then will the flowers, leaves, and grass be as fair, pleasant, and glorious as an emerald, and all creatures be at their fairest.

Even now, when we have God's grace shining on us, all the creatures smile on us.

And in the new heavens there will be a great, eternal light and beauty. What here we would be, there we shall be. Wherever thought takes us, thither the body also will be able to follow.

In this life the body is obedient to the will.

Much more in the future life shall the body be able easily to obey the will. All shall be restored us there, but shining, bright, glorious. And all which here we count fair will be as nothing, by comparison, there. We shall be satisfied with God's grace, and be altogether what we would be. There shall be all that we would so fain have here, namely: justice, peace, joy, blessedness, and we shall be free from all sickness and every evil chance.

To a heart that is full of joy, all it sees is joyful; but to a sad heart all is sad. Change of heart is the greatest change.

All that we lost in Paradise we shall receive again far better, and far more abundantly. The new heavens and earth, each shall be full of the life which belongs to each.

NOT only in heaven shall we be, but wheresoever we will in heaven or earth; no more tottering under this heavy body, which ever drags us earthward. The body itself shall then be full of activity and life.

IT is a great thing to believe that then the weak and burdensome body shall be so vigorous, and swift, and full of life and activity. I believe this but feebly; the world not at all.

If here we have such pleasure in the creatures, in the sun, the stars, and all the creation, what will it be there, where we shall see God face to face?

There the Saints shall keep eternal Holy Day, ever joyful, secure, and free from all suffering; ever satisfied in God.

This body is a Sepulchre.

SLEEP is nothing else than a death, and death a sleep. What is our death but a night's sleep? For as, through sleep all weariness and faintness pass away and cease, and the powers of the spirit come back again, so that in the morning we arise fresh, and strong, and joyous; so at the Last Day we shall rise again, as if we had only slept a night, and shall be fresh and strong.

Wonder of the Saints at the Joy of Heaven.

THOSE who in their necessity and anguish could comfort themselves no otherwise than because they had Christ the Son of God as their Saviour and their Advocate with the Father, by keeping close to His Word, and by a heartfelt yearning and longing for His blessed appearing,—those shall then look with wonder on one another. We shall recognize one another and say, "Lo! verily, do we meet again thus? Who would have foreseen this wonderful, blessed transformation? On earth we were the most miserable, the least esteemed, and sorely tried; were called heretics and those who turned the world upside down, were scorned and mocked, trampled under foot, hunted down, cast into dungeons, slain by torture, sword, and fire. We bore the cross a little while, yea, but for a moment, compared with this great glory which is now revealed in us; and now behold, we live with Christ in unspeakable eternal joy, and praise Him, the Father and the Holy Spirit with all the angels and saints."

"IF we rightly considered," said Doctor Martin, "how great the glory of the future life will be, for which we wait, when we shall rise again from the dead, we should not be so heavy-hearted and unwilling to suffer all kinds of trials, torments, and wrong from this evil world.

"When the Son of Man, our dear Lord Christ, shall come at the Last Day to judge the quick and the dead, and His sentence falls on the godly and on the ungodly, then we shall be ashamed at heart, and each say to himself, 'Shame on thee! Had I indeed believed God's word, I would have suffered gladly not only sore temptation, and unjust imprisonment, but would willingly have been trampled under the feet of all the Turks and the ungodly, and have lain there, for the sake of the coming glory which now I see revealed.'"

GO into the garden and ask the cherry-tree how it is possible that from a dry, dead twig can spring a little, living eye, and from that eye can spring cherries? Go into the house and ask the matron how it is possible that from the lifeless egg can come the living bird?

And since God does such wonders with cherries and with eggs, canst thou not give Him the glory of believing that if He suffers the winter to come over thee, if He suffers thee to die and be imprisoned in the earth, thee also, when His summer comes, will He bring forth again and awaken from the dead?

Christ calling all by Name to Him.

MY Lord is called "*Sit thou at My right hand.*" He saith "I will raise you up again at the last day." And then He will also say, "Doctor Martin, Doctor Jonas, Master Michael Cœli, come hither!" He will call us all by name. Forward then: fear not.

The Advent (as he believed) near.

THE light of the Gospel in our times is a sure sign of the glorious Advent of the Lord Christ. It is like the rose of dawn preceding the Eternal Day, and the rising of the Sun of Righteousness.

THE prophets threw the Advents of Christ together; as now we know that the Last Day will come, yet cannot know what or how things will be after it, except only in general that there will be eternal joy, peace and blessedness. So the prophets held that immediately after the coming of Christ, the Last Day would come. They have also thrown together the signs of the First and Second Advent, as if both would happen at one time.

So also in the Epistle to the Corinthians St. Paul questions whether the Day of Judgment will soon come, while those then at Corinth still lived. And even Christ Himself did the same, placing the signs of both close together.

DOCTOR MARTIN said, "Oh, my God, come at last! I am ever waiting for that Day, early in the spring, when day and night are equal, and there will be a bright clear dawning. These are my thoughts. Quickly from this rosy morning sky, a black, thick cloud will arise, and three flashes of lightning, then a peal of thunder, and in a moment (a 'now,'), in the twinkling of an eye, the heavens and the earth will collapse, smitten into an indistinguishable mass. Praise God who has taught us not to dread, but to sigh and long for that Day. Under the Papacy all the world dreaded it : 'Dies iræ, dies illa.'"

STIEFEL said once, "As I was on the way hither, I saw a glorious rainbow, and I thought of the Last Day." "Nay, it will not come ushered in by rainbows," said Dr. Martin, "but with a sudden crash; with fire, thunder and lightning, the whole creation shall pass away. In a moment we shall all be changed. A mighty trumpet-peal will awaken and renew us all. It will not be the soft sighing of a lute that shall awaken all that are in the graves to hear."

A FAR different pomp from the pomp of the triumphal entry of kings and emperors, will that Advent have. For the whole air shall be full of angels and of saints, who shall shine brighter than the sun.

AT Easter-tide, in April, when there was least fear of rain, Pharaoh perished in the Red Sea and Israel was led out of Egypt.

At the same season the world was created. At that season the year changes; and then Christ arose again and renewed the world.

So, perhaps, at the same season will dawn the Last Day. I have a thought that this Day will come about Easter-tide, when the year is pleasantest and most fair; and early, when the sun ariseth, as with Sodom and Gomorrha.

The heavens will become troubled, and there will be thunders and earthquakes, perhaps for an hour or longer. Then the people who see it will say, "See! see! you foolish creature! Did you never hear thunder before?"

And suddenly the whole world will fall together, and many a debt will remain unpaid.

BY these fires in the sky I judge the Last Day to be at the doors. The empire is falling, kings are falling, priests are falling, the whole world everywhere is falling, even as a great house, when about to fall, is wont first to begin its ruin with little cracks.

His Prayer for the Speedy Advent of Christ.

HELP, O Lord my God, that the joyful Day of Thy Holy Advent may come, that we may be redeemed from this evil, envious world, the Devil's kingdom, and be set free from the bitter torments that we have to suffer both from without and from within, both from wicked men and from our own conscience. Destroy this old Adam, that we may be clothed with another body that is not disposed to evil and excess as this is, but which, redeemed from all infirmity, shall be made like unto Thy glorious body, my Lord Jesus Christ, so that at last we may attain our full and glorious redemption.

Luther's last Conflict and Victory.

ON Wednesday the 17th of February, 1543, it was observed that he was feeble and ailing. The Princes of Anhalt and the Count Albert Mansfeld, with Dr. Jonas and his other friends, entreated him to rest in his own room during the morning. He was not easily persuaded to spare himself, and probably would not have yielded then, had he not felt that the work of reconciliation was accomplished, in all save a few supplementary details. Much of the forenoon, therefore, he reposed on a leathern couch in his room, occasionally rising, with the restlessness of illness, and pacing the room or standing in the window praying, so that Dr. Jonas and Cœlius, who were in another part of the room, could hear him. He dined, however, at noon, in the Great Hall, with those assembled there. At dinner he said to some near him, "If I can, indeed, reconcile the rulers of my birthplace with each other, and then, with God's permission, accomplish the journey back to Wittemberg, I would go home and lay myself down to sleep in my grave, and let the worms devour my body."

IN the afternoon he complained of painful pressure on the breast, and requested that it might be rubbed with warm cloths. This relieved him a little; and he went to supper again with his friends in the Great Hall. At table he spoke much of eternity, and said he believed his own death was near; yet his conversation was not only cheerful, but at times gay, although it related chiefly to the future world. One near him asked whether departed saints would recognize each other in heaven. He said, yes, he thought they would.

WHEN he left the supper-table he went to his room. In the night his two sons,

Paul and Martin, thirteen and fourteen years of age, sat up to watch with Justus Jonas, whose joys and sorrows he had shared through so many years. Cœlius and Aurifaber also were with him. The pain in the breast returned, and again they tried rubbing him with hot cloths. Count Albert came and the Countess, with two physicians, and brought him some shavings from the tusk of a sea-unicorn, deemed a sovereign remedy. He took it, and slept till ten. Then he awoke, and attempted once more to pace the room a little; but he could not and returned to bed. Then he slept again till one. During those two or three hours of sleep, his host Albrecht, with his wife, Ambrose, Jonas, and Luther's son, watched noiselessly beside him, quietly keeping up the fire. Everything depended on how long he slept, and how he woke.

The first words he spoke when he woke sent a shudder of apprehension through their hearts.

He complained of cold, and asked them to pile up more fire. Alas! the chill was creeping over him which no effort of man could remove.

Dr. Jonas asked him if he felt very weak. "Oh," he replied, "how I suffer! My dear Jonas, I think I shall die here, at Eisleben, where I was born and baptized.

His other friends were awakened and brought in to his bedside.

JONAS spoke of the sweat on his brow as a hopeful sign, but Dr. Luther answered:

"It is the cold sweat of death. I must yield up my spirit, for my sickness increaseth."

Then he prayed fervently, saying:

"Heavenly Father, everlasting and merciful God, Thou hast revealed to me Thy dear Son, our Lord Jesus Christ. Him have I taught; Him have I experienced; Him have I confessed; Him I adore and love as my beloved Saviour, Sacrifice, and Redeemer—Him whom the godless persecute, dishonor, and reproach. O heavenly Father, though I must resign my body, and be borne away from this life, I know that I shall be with Him forever. Take my poor soul up to Thee."

Afterwards he took a little medicine, and assuring his friends that he was dying, said three times:

"Father, into Thy hands do I commend my spirit. Thou has redeemed me, Thou faithful God. Truly God hath so loved the world!"

Then he lay quite quiet and motionless. Those around sought to rouse him, and began to rub his chest and limbs, and spoke to him, but he made no reply. Then Jonas and Cœlius, for the solace of the many who had received the truth from his lips, spoke aloud, and said:

"Venerable father, do you die trusting in Christ, and in the doctrine you have constantly preached?"

He answered by an audible and joyful "Yes."

That was his last word on earth. Then turning on his right side, he seemed to fall peaceably asleep for a quarter of an hour. Once more hope awoke in the hearts of his children and his friends; but the physician told them it was no favorable symptom.

A light was brought near his face; a death-like paleness was creeping over it, and his hands and feet were becoming cold.

Gently once more he sighed; and with hands folded on his breast, yielded up his spirit to God without a struggle.

This was at four o'clock in the morning of the 18th of February, 1543.

CPSIA information can be obtained
at www.ICGtesting.com
Printed in the USA
BVHW061806270221
601217BV00005B/351